THE CONCEPT OF NATURE

2002

THE CONCEPT OF NATURE

JOHN HABGOOD

DARTON · LONGMAN + TODD

2002 ·

To my grandchildren, in the hope that
they will appreciate, and cherish,
the wonders of God's creation.

First published in 2002 by
Darton, Longman and Todd Ltd
1 Spencer Court
140–142 Wandsworth High Street
London SW18 4JJ

ISBN 0–232–52439–4

A catalogue record for this book is available from the British Library.

Designed by Sandie Boccacci
Phototypeset in 10.25/13pt Sabon
by Intype London Ltd
Printed and bound in Great Britain by
The Bath Press, Bath

CONTENTS

ACKNOWLEDGEMENTS

I am grateful to the University of Aberdeen for the invitation to deliver the Gifford Lectures 2000, which form the basis of this book, and for the warm hospitality provided to a visiting lecturer. I wish to thank also those many authors from whose writings I have learnt and quoted, and especially Faber and Faber for permission to quote from poems by Seamus Heaney and Edwin Muir, and Curtis Brown, on behalf of the Isaiah Berlin Literary Trust, for permission to quote Isaiah Berlin. In addition I acknowledge my debt to other publishers whose failure to answer letters I interpret as tacit permission to quote their authors.

I also want to thank my friend and former colleague, Raymond Barker who, not for the first time, helped me by reading the whole manuscript and making many valuable suggestions.

INTRODUCTION

In 1885 an elderly Scottish judge, Lord Gifford, endowed a lectureship in each of the four ancient Scottish universities for 'Promoting, Advancing, Teaching and Diffusing the study of Natural Theology'. By Natural Theology he had in mind the open rational exploration of all matters to do with the knowledge of God. The emphasis was on the word 'open'. Lecturers were not required to subscribe to any particular belief, nor expected to appeal to any particular revelation. The Lectures began in 1888, and for more than a hundred years have been astonishingly fertile in generating scholarly discussion of this most important of all issues. Sometimes they have been too scholarly, and have drawn correspondingly small and specialised audiences. This is why in recent years the emphasis has reverted to another stipulation in Lord Gifford's will, namely that they should be 'public and popular discourses ... open not only to students of the Universities, but to the whole community without matriculation'.

Though Gifford Lectures are still intended to be a serious contribution to knowledge, it is no longer necessary for them to be heavily academic. I have been one of the beneficiaries of the change, in that it has been my unusual privilege to deliver Gifford Lectures in two of the four universities. On the first occasion, in 1988, it was only a single lecture in the University of Glasgow, as part of the series to mark the centenary. Other lecturers in that series included such academics far removed from orthodox theology as Richard Dawkins and Don Cupitt.[1] A subsequent invitation to deliver the millennium series in the University of

[ix]

Aberdeen was the origin of this book. The delivery of the six lectures, of which this is a greatly expanded version, happened to coincide with the floods and rail disruptions of November 2000, but the warmth of hospitality in the University made up for much miserable travelling.

I had a personal reason for choosing *The Concept of Nature* as my theme, apart from its obvious relevance to many of the contentious issues of our time. In the late 1940s, when I was a research student in neurophysiology, I decided that I ought to embark on a serious study of the Christian faith. I had no idea where to start, so I browsed in the theological section of a Cambridge bookshop, spotted a name I recognised – William Temple – and bought a fat volume, *Nature, Man and God*,[2] whose title seemed to me comprehensive enough to meet all my needs. It was Temple's Gifford Lectures, delivered between 1932 and 1934 – a five hundred page exercise in philosophical theology, and an astonishing achievement for a man who at the time was Archbishop of York. He is said to have written them in odd half-hours late at night. Re-reading the book fifty years later, I have been struck by how much of it influenced my own thinking about the foundations of faith. Nor can I escape the coincidence that, to the best of my knowledge, I am the only other archbishop to follow in his footsteps as a Gifford Lecturer.

But I have also been struck by the extent to which present-day concerns about nature are totally absent from the book, perhaps not surprisingly, given the huge differences between our own world and that of the 1930s. More worryingly it is hard to know what Temple actually meant by the word 'nature', unless it simply stood for all that exists, apart from humanity and God. As a philosopher much influenced by idealism, he liked to stress the relationship between what he called 'Mind' and the 'World Process'. This appears occasionally in such delphic utterances as 'If, as science has disclosed, Mind is part of Nature, then Nature must be grounded in Mind.'[3] It is not the sort of sentence which immediately strikes a chord with modern readers.

Apart from such passing references to nature and science, there is also a notable absence in his lectures of any discussion of the natural sciences in their own right. Indeed Temple is said to have claimed that his ignorance of science was so profound as to be distinguished. I may thus be able to repay my debt to him, and at the same time hope to satisfy Lord Gifford's intentions, by looking more closely at the word in his title which Temple, for the most part, ignored.

Mary Midgley[4] has used the analogy of plumbing to describe this kind of exploration. In any ordinary house there is usually a great deal which lies hidden and is apt to be taken for granted unless something manifestly goes wrong. In old houses the plumbing system may have grown haphazardly over the years as new facilities have been added, and it may not be at all obvious how it was once meant to work, where the blockages might be, and why the whole thing judders when a certain tap is opened. There is a need for specialist attention; and it can be the same with concepts. They too may grow imperceptibly as meanings are added or circumstances change, and may likewise need specialist attention if the flow of thought which depends on them is not to be distorted or obstructed. This is Midgley's defence of professional philosophy. But even ordinary householders can make a contribution, if only by knowing from occasional forays under the floorboards where the pipes actually go. I am not a philosopher, and modern archbishops do not have time to be specialists. In the course of a lifetime, though, I have had to look under the floorboards, as it were, in many unlikely places, and it is this varied experience which underlies my attempt at an elementary piece of map-work.

Chapter 1 explores the multiple meanings of the word 'nature', traces some of their origins, and classifies them broadly under three main heads – nature as referring to the essential characteristics of a thing, nature as a force which makes things what they are, and nature as a description of everything that is. Under each of these headings there are further questions to be asked about what is given in the way things are, and what is socially constructed.

Chapter 2 centres on the use of the word in the natural sciences, and questions the assumptions underlying a purely

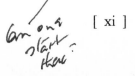

naturalistic approach to the description of reality. A god-like perspective on the world of nature as a whole is not available to us.

Chapter 3 considers environmental issues. Given the extent to which human beings have always shaped their environment, is there a 'natural world' to be conserved or a 'balance of nature' to be respected? And is there a convincing intellectual basis for environmentalism?

Chapter 4 takes up the much-disputed theme of whether there is a natural moral law of universal application. It is suggested that while there may not be universal laws, there may be universal values to which appeal can be made. The frequent reference to what is deemed to be 'natural' in the context of sexuality is used as a test case of whether the concept has any clear meaning in the field of morality.

Chapter 5 describes how human beings have constantly tried to improve nature, whether by artistry as in landscaping, or for more utilitarian purposes as in breeding programmes, and asks how far our massively increased powers of manipulation, mainly nowadays through genetics, require new ethical constraints.

Chapter 6 draws together these various themes around the ideas of givenness and potentiality, and relates them to traditional beliefs about God. The book concludes with a discussion of nature and grace, and suggests that, far from being in antithesis to one another, nature may have incarnational significance as a means through which the grace of God can be discerned and received.

ONE

WORDS AND THINGS

An immediate problem with the word 'nature' is that it has multiple and overlapping meanings. If I were to write, 'A Gifford lecturer might naturally be expected to talk about the nature of Nature, given the lectureship's emphasis on natural theology, even though mere human nature is not equal to the task,' any sensitive reader would rightly be repelled by the apparent conceptual muddle. Nevertheless it should not be too difficult to grasp my meaning, despite the fact that 'nature' is used in five different senses in the same sentence. Context can tell us a great deal about the shade of meaning intended, but it cannot do so, or filter out unintended associations, unless there is some initial clarity about what the different meanings are. So let me begin with a brief look at these five.

What a Gifford lecturer might 'naturally' be expected to talk about is something which clearly fits in with the intention of the lectureship itself. 'Natural' in this context means 'obvious', 'appropriate', 'what might be expected in the circumstances'. These are all variations on a more general sense of the word in which the 'natural' is what belongs to the ordinary world, or to an ordinary way of life, and is hence customary. In short, what we have here is an extension of the concept of the natural in the direction of 'common usage', until it becomes virtually indistinguishable from what is culturally familiar. Thus 'doing what comes naturally' may hint at some deep relationship with reality, or it may just mean following the fashion.

The next phrase, 'the nature of Nature' is a literary

monstrosity, but it illustrates the point that there needs to be a clear contrast between meanings. To ask about the 'nature' of something is to ask what kind of a thing it is, what are its essential characteristics. Those who enjoy tracing links between words can note how 'kind' comes from 'kin', and 'nature' from *natus* or birth. Thus, according to this meaning, the nature of a thing is what is innate to it, what makes it what it is.

The other half of the phrase, the Nature whose nature we are considering, refers not just to a quality or kind, but to a wide variety of other things. At one extreme it can include everything that exists, the whole natural world; sometimes this 'everything' is held to include humanity, and sometimes not. In other contexts it might mean country rather than town, or the environment, or the world as left to itself in contrast with the world as shaped by humanity. It can also describe a force or guiding principle, Nature doing this or that, Mother Nature operating her own laws and thus determining the way things are.

My fourth use of the word, as in 'natural theology', picks up some of these meanings, and contrasts what can be known by reflection on the evidence of the senses with what claims to be revealed by God. There are similarities here to the contrast between the natural sciences and the human sciences, where 'natural' refers to what is claimed to be objective and universal, as opposed to what is subjective and personal.

The fifth meaning, as in 'human nature' might seem a repeat of the second, when I referred to the 'nature' of Nature. But in fact there is a subtle difference. Usually when people talk about human nature they have in mind particular quirks and characteristics which make people interesting. They are not so much concerned with what kind of thing an individual human being is, but with what human beings are like, and how they behave, and why it is normal, for instance, for most ordinary human beings to become restive during discussions about mere words.

So there we have it – five meanings in one rather unnatural sentence. An American scholar is said to have identified more than a hundred shades of meaning. But five is perhaps enough, and if one really tries, one can reduce the main variants to three, all of which had their origin in ancient Greece.[1]

CLASSICAL BEGINNINGS

The most primitive meaning of 'nature' in both Greek and Latin seems to have been 'the character or quality of something'. It is the answer to the question, what kind of a thing is it? In Greek the word is *'phusis'*, and in Latin *'natura'*. *Phusis* is the origin of our word 'physics', the study of the nature of things, and like *natura*, seems to have been derived from the word for being born. Hence it can carry the meaning 'the way things are by virtue of their coming to be'. This is the first meaning, and it is still much in use. It can be extended in the direction of 'ordinary' to include the idea of 'doing what comes naturally' referred to earlier.

The second meaning represents a move in the direction of generalisation. It is not difficult to see how the idea that each thing has its own nature might lead to the coalescence of these various natures into a single nature, or endowment, or directive force, which is common to them all. It is a movement of thought which was more likely to take place in a literate culture with the beginnings of an educational system, than in a non-literate one. Literacy makes it easier to build on individual experience, and thus to draw together multiple stories, insights and experiences into an ordered whole.[2] One of the great achievements of classical Greece was to pioneer these more systematic ways of thinking by developing concepts which had some claim to be universal. Hence 'nature' in its second sense no longer referred simply to the concrete natures of actual things but could become the subject of natural philosophy, the study of that which makes everything what it is. This is a more abstract and generalised concept of nature, suitable for being dignified with a capital N.

It is plausible to suggest a parallel with what happened in the emergence of ideas about God, since it was not only in Greece that the growth of literacy changed the way people thought. Religions, too, during the widespread intellectual ferment of the

[3]

fifth and fourth centuries B.C., began to become more sys-
tematised. Encounters with the god or spirit of this place or that
place, or this event or that event, tended to give way to a more
unified experience in a more unified cosmos. People might still
refer respectfully to individual gods, but these began to be over-
shadowed by awareness of a reality transcending time, place,
and particularity, God as a proper name, with a capital G. In
the biblical tradition the great prophetic assertions about the
transcendent unity of God belong to the time when the words
of the prophets actually began to be written down, and were
part of the process whereby numerous myths, stories, and sayings
began to be incorporated into a literary tradition.[3] It is perhaps
no coincidence that it was also an age of great empires, in which
people had to live and think under the pressure of events
which impinged on much more than their own tribe, nation or
locality.

Whatever the precise reasons, the Classical Age began the
search for intellectual coherence, and the concept of Nature as a
unifying force, an energising ground of things, was one way of
expressing the intelligibility of the universe. It became possible
to talk about Nature doing this or that, and even to personify
it, as in the phrase 'Mother Nature' which clearly has religious
overtones, albeit pagan ones. When centuries later Marcus Aurelius expressed the typically Stoic thought, 'since the universal
Nature has made rational animals for the sake of one another . . .
he who transgresses her will is clearly guilty of impiety towards
the highest divinity,' it was this personification of the natural
order of things which he must have been assuming.[4] At a still
later stage the idea of Nature as somehow the underlying reality
or cause of things could undergird the concept of the laws of
nature, whether scientific or moral. 'Nature teaches us . . .' we
say, the assumption being that it is indeed a unity. Or when
Byron wrote, 'The fault was Nature's fault not thine, which made
thee fickle as thou art',[5] it is this second sense of some directive
or pervasive force he seems to have had in mind.

The third meaning of 'nature' is simply 'the entire physical
world'. As I have already pointed out, it is not always clear

whether human beings are to be included in this or not. Obviously our bodies are part of the physical world, yet in certain respects we also stand outside it, able to observe and study it, and to characterise it as physical. In fact there is plenty of room for confusion here, as there seems to have been in the origin of the notion itself.

The Greeks are said to have been the first to give the same name, *phusis*, to the whole of physical reality, as well as to the unifying power which they saw as underlying that reality, and to the particular character of each part of it. However, it is only in the last few centuries that this sense of 'nature' as the whole physical world has become predominant, largely coinciding with the rise of the natural sciences. How and why the extension of meaning originally occurred in classical thought cannot be pinpointed precisely. It may nevertheless be useful to look back in a little more detail at some of the key factors in the emergence of all three concepts of nature, and especially of this most comprehensive meaning.

ARISTOTELIAN SCIENCE

Aristotle tells us how the earliest Greek philosophers, the Ionians, drew the distinction between things human beings had made, and things which occurred by themselves – in other words, between artefacts and natural objects. They assumed that what was common to all natural things was that they were made of a single substance. As Aristotle later saw it, the universal substance was differentiated into countless natural forms, each according to its own *phusis*. This was a clear use of the first sense of *phusis* as essence, or more precisely, *phusis* as those characteristics of a thing on which all its other properties depend. To have the *phusis* of a bird, for instance, is to have feathers, wings, two legs, etc., in fact all those observable features by which we can recognise that what we are encountering is actually a bird.

The efforts of these early philosophers, though, were directed, not towards investigating these individual natures, which might have spelt the beginnings of natural science, but in speculations about what the single universal substance underlying them might be.[6] Whereas Aristotle asked what everything was for – as in his oft-repeated remark 'whatever Nature makes she makes for some purpose'[7] (or 'Nature does nothing in vain') – *their* primary question was 'What is it made of?' As Aristotle himself put it,

> Some hold that the nature and substantive existence of natural products resides in their materials . . . this is why some have said that it was earth that constituted the nature of things, some fire, some air, some water . . . for whichever substance or substances each thinker assumed to be primary, he regarded as constituting the existence of all things in general . . .[8]

Their speculations led nowhere, because all suffered from the fatal defect that if the underlying universal substance was already known in its basic form, how could one explain its differentiation into other forms totally unlike it? If everything is ultimately made of water, how can one explain the difference between water and rocks? If we then ask why they pursued this hopeless quest, the answer must surely lie in the strength of the new awareness that there must be some kind of underlying unity beneath the dazzling multiplicity and complexity of the world as experienced. But their conviction was premature. The only thing they succeeded in demonstrating was that there are no short cuts to discovering what the underlying unity might be.

Their successors, the Pythagorean philosophers, took a huge step forward by explaining the differences between things in terms of their structure. Curiously enough, it was music which provided the clue. They reflected on the fact that the differences between musical notes from a single vibrating string depend on the length of the string. There is a simple mathematical relationship between them; the shorter the string the higher the note. Here then was a difference in quality which could be accounted for by a difference in quantity. It is not too much of an exaggeration to say that in this mathematical discovery lay the seeds of all future science. If the ultimate nature of things depends on mathematical relationships, then it follows that the world as perceived by our senses must be as logical and intelligible as mathematics. Reality, in short, is rational.

To discern this rationality we need to know what things actually exist, and to distinguish their different natures. This was one of Aristotle's great contributions. It is to him that we owe the first detailed study of what we now call the natural world, which was for him essentially a living world. 'Some things exist, or come into existence, by nature; some otherwise. Animals and their organs, plants, and the elementary substances – earth, air, fire, water – these and their likes we say exist by nature ... the common feature that characterises them all seems to be that they have within them a principle of movement and rest . . .'[9] Nature, in other words – the sub-lunary world of movement and change – was to be contrasted with the heavens which were unchanging, as well as with those unchanging elements which underlay all change in the world, namely matter or substance. The potentially changeable form of each thing, was its *phusis*.

In his *Metaphysics* Aristotle further explored seven possible definitions of *phusis*,[10] and finally declared its fundamental meaning to be 'the essence of things which have a source of movement in themselves'. All living moving things, animals in short, and to a lesser extent vegetables, are natural and have their own *phusis*. The non-living elements of the world, mountains and rocks and houses for instance, have no source of movement, or internal organising principle, within themselves, but have had their form imposed on them by some external agency, as in human artefacts. A bed, for instance, may be made of wood, which has its own inner organisation or form, and is to that extent natural. But the bed as such has no organising principle within itself, nor will it move by itself, and if planted in the ground will not sprout baby beds. If it were capable of sprouting anything it would sprout a tree, because what persists is the essential natural quality of a thing, in this instance the wood of which it was made.

Given his definition of nature as essentially organic, we can see why Aristotle was not so interested in the material constitution of things, in fact was notoriously vague about the meaning of matter and substance. As an example of the confusion, he casually remarks at one point '. . . the term *phusis* is used rightly in two senses (a) meaning "matter" and (b) meaning "essence" . . .'.[11] The implication here seems to be that the nature of something is the substantial existence of the thing itself, as well as the form and characteristics which make it what it is. It would be unfair to blame him too much for not being clear. The concept of substance is notorious for the intractable problems to which it gives rise – problems which, as we shall see in the next chapter, are no less intractable when pursued with all the armoury of modern physics. It is often the simplest questions which are the hardest, and the question, What is matter? is one of them.

Be that as it may, what really interested Aristotle were the causes of things. From his definition of *phusis* as 'the essence of things which have a source of movement in themselves' it is but a short step to believing that natural processes are inherently directed towards goals. Living things move for a purpose. Hence to explain their behaviour it is necessary to think in terms of so-called 'final causes', i.e. causes which specify goals and purposes, as well as the, to him, less interesting 'efficient causes' – efficient because they have knock-on effects, as when one billiard ball hits another.

There is a famous example of the relationship between final and efficient causes in Aristotle's description of human hair.

> Man has the hairiest head among all animals. There are two reasons for this: 1. The brain is fluid, and the skull has many sutures. A large outgrowth is bound to appear where there is a large amount of fluid and hot substance. 2. On purpose to give protection; that is the hair affords shelter both from excessive cold and from excessive heat. The human brain is the biggest and most fluid of all brains: therefore it needs the greatest amount of protection. A very fluid thing is very liable both to violent heating and violent cooling.[12]

The passage is interesting, first because it was picked on by Sir Francis Bacon in his tirade against final causes, but secondly because, while the efficient cause suggested by Aristotle is clearly absurd, the final cause appears to make a good deal of sense. Hair does indeed protect the head, though not for the precise reason Aristotle suggests. But though it has a purpose, in a Darwinian world we now know that the idea of purpose is not necessary in order to explain its existence.

For a less bizarre example, consider a salmon trying to reach its spawning ground, as it persistently tries to jump up and over seemingly impassable obstacles, even to the jeopardy of its own life. It may seem obvious to a spectator that the salmon is pursuing a goal. Its behaviour can be understood in terms of a final cause, its desire to reproduce. Modern reductionist biological orthodoxy, however, would be highly suspicious of any such form of explanation. The salmon is not consciously or unconsciously pursuing anything. It is thrashing about responding to chemical signals in the water itself, which have the effect of causing it to move upstream. The salmon's movements, it is claimed, can be explained wholly in terms of efficient causes, a pattern of chemical reactions which, after evolving in a fairly stable environment, have resulted in a successful, albeit complex, method of breeding. The appearance of goal-directed behaviour, from this perspective, is as illusory as the idea that a billiard ball deliberately seeks its pocket. Within a reductionist understanding of science, which seeks to explain all phenomena in terms of the behaviour of their most fundamental constituents, only efficient causes are acceptable. While this may be a helpful approach in the study of salmon, given what is now known about the mental limitations of fish, it may not seem to give much insight into the various moves and counter-moves as a lion stalks it prey, and still less into our own intentional activities, when we are conscious of having a goal clearly in mind. It is therefore worth digressing a little to look more closely at how far sophisticated goal-directed behaviour can actually be explained away as something else.

For a much less ambiguous example than that of hair or salmon, think of a robot designed to search for water on Mars. Its behaviour is undoubtedly goal-directed, yet also fully explicable in terms of the multiple operations taking place within its electrical circuitry.[13] Goal-directed behaviour, in other words, does not require the existence of a mysterious extra something in the machine itself. It does, however, imply that at some point somebody has made a decision about what the machine is for. Similar appearances of goal-directed behaviour in animals, and even in human beings, may likewise be explicable in terms of what is happening in the circuitry of the brain, though the possibilities of being able to tease out in any detail precisely what is going on at this fundamental level are exceedingly remote. In the absence of such detailed demonstration, or even of the serious prospect of it, the assertion that, despite appearances, there is nothing more to thinking and deciding than a huge number of highly complex physical events, is sustained by the assumption that such explanation is in principle possible. Maybe so. But even with a relatively simple robot, it is doubtful whether an explanation at the level of circuitry can supersede other types of explanation in terms of what the robot was designed to do. Even to understand the circuitry, there needs to be some inkling of how and why it is supposed to operate, quite apart from its larger purpose in the human scheme of things. In fact all discussion of goals, and goal-directed behaviour, assumes a context more extensive than that of the individual animal or machine whose inner workings are under investigation. Or to put it in Aristotelian terms, the concept of final causes still has relevance at the level at which life is actually lived, and hence by implication also for systems at a lower level of being. Thus even in a robot it may not be necessary to regard final and efficient causes as mutually exclusive.

As an example of a goal-directed system, Aristotle invites us to consider the human hand. The purpose of fingers, he says, is incomprehensible apart from the purpose of the whole hand. The point can be generalised by saying that the understanding of the whole of a system may be necessary for an understanding of the operations of its parts. Indeed it is possible to go further and say that just as the whole depends on the operation of each of its parts, so each part depends on the operation of the whole. Thus the movements of each finger, though individually controlled, are also interdependent and have to relate to what the hand as a whole is doing. Causality, in other words, even at this relatively simple level, has to be interpreted in a wider context, which takes into account the purpose of the whole system.

While this may be true as far as it goes, Aristotle's example is likely to sound strange to modern ears. In describing the purpose of hands and fingers, a more usual starting point these days might be to set them in an evolutionary context, just as one might describe human hair as an evolutionary left-over. One could trace the way in which hands and fingers evolved together with no clear goal in view, as the paws and claws from which they developed gradually acquired new uses. But Aristotle was surely right to see that, as they now exist, hand and fingers can only be understood in relation to one another, and that on a much larger scale the purposeful combination of different functions is found *par excellence* in the human person as a whole. Our human experience of highly co-ordinated and goal-directed activity is fundamental to what we are. If it is dismissed as an incidental and insignificant epiphenomenon in a universe which does not need the concept of purpose, we may be losing a vital category for understanding the nature of things as a whole. The point is not that final causes have somehow to be smuggled back into science; rather that different types or levels of explanation are appropriate for different purposes, and can happily co-exist. But this is to anticipate. It is a difficult and contentious subject, to which I shall be returning in the next chapter.

Meanwhile the point of this digression has been to suggest that if we are to understand what Aristotle meant by *phusis*, it is essential not to dismiss his concept of final causes too summarily, particularly when thinking about complex organic systems. As he saw it, the nature of each living thing could only be understood in terms of the goals for which it existed. For him it was inherent in the *phusis* of each thing that it should go through a process of development until it reached the final and perfect *phusis* for which it was intended – a quasi-theological idea which also has moral implications, as we shall see in Chapter 4.

One important practical consequence of this belief was the collection of huge quantities of apparently unrelated biological facts, as part of an attempt to identify the essential nature and purpose of each species. The particular characteristics of birds, for instance, can only make sense in terms of a bird's ability to fly, and its whole process of development may be seen as directed towards that end. One of Aristotle's more famous studies was a day-by-day observation of hens' eggs during the process of incubation, probably the first ever systematic study of embryology.[14] He concluded from it, erroneously as it turned out, that the heart is the first organ to be formed, and that this must be so because it is the seat of life itself. Many other conclusions were similarly mistaken, a hardly surprising result in view of the fact that he was the first to undertake any such attempt at systematic classification. But in the context of the development of ideas about nature it is significant for two reasons. First, it was a pioneering attempt to study the natural world in detail and as a whole, and hence an important step in the extension of the meaning of 'nature' to include everything. Secondly, despite its manifold deficiencies, it paved the way for what we now call Natural History, which in turn became the essential foundation on which modern biological knowledge is built.

Aristotle's dictum 'nature does nothing in vain' was also capable of bearing unexpected fruit. He implied by it that, in addition to the purposiveness of individual organs and organisms, there is a more general purposiveness in the natural world as a whole. 'Nature', he wrote, 'like an intelligent human being, always assigns each organ to something that is capable of using it . . .'[15] Only intelligent creatures, for instance, have hands, because only intelligent creatures can use them appropriately. This wider use of *phusis* as a force or guiding principle points to 'nature' in our second sense, as energising and perhaps directing the world towards that fullness and vitality within which each individual nature is to be realised. It was an idea with deep roots in Greek culture, in which it was common to think of the natural world as a single organism, and even to ascribe to it some sort of soul. In a later Christian context it gave birth to natural theology, in particular the argument for God's existence from the evidence for design in the natural world –

only, as it was then thought, capable of being explained by some directing intelligence.

Alternatively, read in a slightly different way, the dictum 'nature does nothing in vain', rather than expressing Aristotle's belief in final causes, might almost be a statement of Darwinian principles. The very basis of evolutionary theory is the belief that the various organs and capacities of living things have developed only because they promote survival. In Aristotelian terms one might say that survival is the final cause of the nature of all that evolves. The theory of evolution sets each individual life within the context of all the interactions between living things as a whole, and it is this widening of context which, as we have seen earlier, may give at least the appearance of purposiveness. Furthermore the forces which have shaped the hugely complex biological world are intelligible, if not intelligent, and it is not absurd to think of natural forces as somehow geared to the evolutionary emergence of intelligence itself. Absurd or not, this is the assumption which fuels the expectations of those who nowadays hope to find intelligent life in other parts of the universe. It is an article of faith among them that, if life once starts, more complex forms of it must inevitably follow, wherever there is a physical environment capable of sustaining them.

Whether or not it is possible to rescue Aristotle from being of merely antiquarian interest by such Darwinian reinterpretation may seem like an academic irrelevance. In terms of the development of the concept of nature, however, the relevant point is that his, and our, second use of the word 'nature', as a force or principle, was clearly implicit in the idea that nature has goals. For the goals to be achievable, there have to be reliable, consistent, and hence rational, laws controlling the mode of operation of nature's forces. Furthermore, as I have indicated previously, in order to identify the goals there has to be systematic study of all aspects of the living, moving, world. Thus if the moving force within the world is a rationally comprehensible *phusis*, and if everything has its own *phusis*, or essence, and if sometimes even the basic substance of things is *phusis*, the question arises, how should one describe the world as a whole? The unity and rationality of the whole was already safeguarded by Aristotle's idea of God as the prime mover in whose activity all the different forms of moving things have their logical ground. For some of his successors it must have seemed but a short step from describing particular things in terms of their *phusis*, to describing everything as *phusis*. But Aristotle himself seems not to have used the word in this comprehensive sense.

Whatever the route by which it happened, the step was taken, and this third all-inclusive meaning of 'nature' came into use, and now predominates. In its wake have followed all manner of subsidiary questions about the different senses in which phenomena can properly be described as part of nature. In common usage today the word frequently refers to the living world as opposed to the non-living, as in the phrase 'natural history'. Or it can mean the natural world, supposedly unsullied by human interference, in contrast with the artificiality of human culture. This is a selling point for so-called natural products, from yoghurt to non-GM foods. The permutations are endless. The main point, though, is that, unless some distinctions are made, 'nature' as a description of everything ceases to have any significant meaning, except as an assertion that there is nothing which cannot be included under the same general description. If nature is everything, nothing can be unnatural, still less super-natural, and even the artificial only seems to be so because we wrongly regard our own actions as falling within a special category. Thus the way is open to a thoroughgoing naturalism, in which everything can be included within the same kind of study, and made subject to the same kind of explanation.

NATURE – GIVEN OR CONSTRUCTED?

I have said enough about ancient uses to prepare the ground for some of the themes which will follow later, and I have suggested how they might have been related. It seems to me that the common thread running through all the meanings of nature I have been describing is a sense of givenness. Thus, according to the first meaning, the essential nature of a thing comprises all those qualities and characteristics which always belong to it, simply given in the way things are. In a world which knew nothing of evolution, such natures could be regarded as fixed.

Nature in its second meaning, as a principle or force, describes the way things happen, and this too is fixed. True, there are ways of speaking, as when people describe struggling against the forces of nature, or when environmentalists claim that we should go with the grain of nature, which might seem to imply that nature in this sense is somehow malleable. But in strict logic this cannot be so. If the laws of nature are fixed, there is no alternative to going with its grain; its laws can be harnessed by us, but not broken by us. Nevertheless there is a looser sense in which people speak of pitting natural forces against one another, and a further sense in which the 'nature' whose forces are to be respected, refers to what was there before human beings started interfering with it. Different forms of complementary and alternative medicine, for instance, appear to use language about the grain of nature, in both our meanings of the word. Much is made of the idea of the wisdom of the body, and the balances within nature which need to be maintained. Indeed there are good scientific grounds for supposing that such balances are important. One of the earliest pioneers in physiology, Claude Bernard, coined the word 'homeostasis' to refer to the complex means by which our internal environment, i.e. the fluids in which all our cells are bathed, is maintained in a constant state despite huge variations in the environment external to our bodies. The maintenance of body temperature in mammals is an obvious example. In fact life itself is only possible because natural forces can be harnessed against one another to maintain islands of stability in a sea of change. But in recognising and seeking to support such natural balances, complementary and alternative forms of medicine also characteristically reject what is deemed to be artificial. They are commonly promoted through phrases like 'going with the flow', 'using nature's remedies', avoiding 'chemicals', etc. Different concepts of what might be meant by the givenness of natural forces underlie these two meanings of nature, and this is why the appeal to what is 'natural' in these particular forms of medicine, as in many other spheres of life, can be a source of confusion.

Nature in its third and most comprehensive sense, meaning the whole physical universe, also has the quality of sheer givenness. It is simply there, the given reality within which our lives have to be lived. 'The world is everything that is the case,' wrote Wittgenstein.[16] But are we who observe it also part of 'the case', or do we at least in some sense stand outside it? Even if we include ourselves wholly within it, we have to reckon with the fact that human beings have never been content with things simply as given. The world we inhabit is to a large extent a humanly constructed world, both physically and mentally. We have changed the face of nature, but we have also interpreted it, in all three meanings of the word, in ways which conform to our own beliefs and desires.

Bishop Butler who wrote perceptively about human foibles and the misunderstandings to which the concept nature can give rise, famously went on to say 'Things and actions are what they are, and the consequences of them will be what they will be: why then should we desire to be deceived?'[17] But, of course, we do. Or if not to be deceived, at least to exercise our own judgement, to ask our own questions, and if need be to make our own mistakes. It is small wonder then that a concept with such a broad and ambivalent range of applications should have spun off out of control, proliferating into a hundred or more shades of meaning, some of them fortunately now obsolete.

Take a few extreme examples. Sir Leicester Dedlock in the novel *Bleak House* was a Baronet surpassing all others in the length of his lineage and the sense of his own importance. Dickens wrote of him, 'He would on the whole admit Nature to be a good idea (a little low, perhaps, when not enclosed with a park fence), but an idea dependent for its execution on your great county families.'[18] For Sir Leicester, Nature was precisely what was *not* given, but what had been suitably refined for refined natures like his own. In similar fashion, when we admire nature nowadays, much of what we admire is what we or our forebears have cultivated.

A second example. In the period immediately after the First World War the most vicious attacks on Einstein's theory of relativity came from a group who called themselves German Natural Philosophers. Their diatribes against him centred on the 'Jewish nature' of relativity. Thus when Hitler came to power in 1933, a former Nobel Prize winner wrote in the official Nazi newspaper:

> The most important example of the dangerous influence of Jewish circles on the study of nature has been provided by Herr Einstein with his mathematically botched up theories consisting of some ancient knowledge and a few arbitrary additions. This theory now gradually falls to pieces, as is the fate of all ideas that are estranged from nature.[19]

'Nature' in this last sentence carries clear overtones from the kind of nature philosophy which was part and parcel of the folk mythology of blood and soil, on which Nazism fed. Here then is a racial interpretation of how 'nature' is to be understood, politicised to confirm some deep-rooted prejudices. There was an equally notorious politicisation of science in the post-war Soviet Union, when orthodox genetics was overthrown in order to promote the highly contentious belief that acquired characteristics can be inherited – in conformity with Marxist theory. Nature was supposed to behave as scientific Marxism said it should, but failed to do so. Trofim Lysenko, the Soviet biologist whose falsified experimental results led to this debacle, presided over a disaster for Soviet agriculture between 1948 and 1964. This was done with the full backing of the Central Committee which had decreed his theory's correctness, and had dismissed or liquidated his scientific opponents.

I take a third example from Hamlet, whose father's ghost describes his own murder as 'most foul, strange, and unnatural'. One wonders what a natural murder would be. We are obviously moving here in the realm of social convention where a murder within a family is deemed to be especially shocking, despite the fact that a high proportion of murders do actually take place within families. 'Natural' in this context presumably has overtones of natural affection, natural loyalties, and natural duties.

As with Sir Leicester Dedlock, it has become an almost wholly cultural concept.

Thus in each of these uses of the concept there is a strong element of social conditioning. One could cite hundreds more in which the three basic meanings of 'nature' are moralised or politicised. Nature is invoked to support a claim that there is some kind of givenness or constraint operating in the moral or political sphere in which the user of the word wants to exercise control. That nature has been tamed by Dickens's great land-owner, is visible evidence of his power. In Nazi philosophy nature will not yield up her secrets to the alien theories of a man whose race marks him off as essentially sub-human, not a natural member of the German people. In Soviet agriculture a natural process of generation had to be made to conform to Marxist dogma, because Marxism is the ultimate, all-embracing science. In Hamlet the givenness of a human relationship has been foully set aside at the behest of pathological lust and ambition.

There is certainly a common thread, tending to imply a degree of givenness, in the use of the word 'nature' in these examples. But it is overlaid, at least in the first three examples, by the use of language as an exercise of power. To suppose that by constant alertness to similar misuses, one might be able to strip away the envelope of social conditioning, and thereby return to the pure essence of the meaning of nature, free of all confusions, would be seriously to misunderstand the way language works. It would be to mistake the clarity of a concept for the untidy and ambivalent reality to which it is intended to refer.

In fact what is usually meant by nature is precisely this con-fused array of overlapping experiences and types of experience, through which the awareness of a reality 'out there' impinges on us and resonates with some of the things we know about our-selves. What those things are that we have to come to terms with as given, and how they are affected by the way we understand them and treat them, will be the subject of the chapters which follow.[20] Meanwhile I end this chapter with a question. Why, despite such ambivalence, does it still matter that we should try to be clear what we mean when we invoke the concept of nature, or react to what we deem to be natural or unnatural?

WHY CLARITY MATTERS

The short answer is that when a concept is so multi-faceted, as well as being so heavily loaded with moral and political baggage, it can merely compound the problems its use is intended to address.

I can attempt a longer answer by describing briefly one of the tasks which I have on hand, and which raises a multitude of questions about how far it is right to go in adapting the natural world to our own ends.

For the past four years or so I have been Chairman of a Department of Health committee charged with responsibility for overseeing all matters to do with xenotransplantation.[21] This is an, as yet, largely untried method designed to meet the increasing shortage of human tissues and organs for transplant surgery, by the use of animal tissues and organs – notably those from pigs. It is a complex subject, involving animal welfare, the safety and effectiveness of radically new procedures, and the unquantifiable risks of unleashing new forms of infection which, if HIV/AIDS and BSE are any guide, might spread to epidemic proportions. All this is set against a background of people dying, or living miserable lives, say, on kidney dialysis, for lack of suitable transplant organs. I will not go into details, except to spell out a further factor in the equation – the so-called yuk factor. Many people, and not just those who are repelled by the subject of animal experimentation in general, feel that it offends deeply 'against nature' to contemplate using animals, and especially pigs, for transplantation into human beings.

There are two main aspects to this yuk factor. They can both be illustrated by one of the techniques which, it is hoped, could eventually make the transplantation of animal organs into human patients feasible. Animal organs or tissues transplanted directly into a host of another species are almost immediately rejected by the host's immune system. But if the source animal is genetically modified by the insertion of the appropriate human gene, this immediate and violent rejection can be prevented. Other forms of immunological reaction may follow, but at least the first hurdle has been overcome. The technique has been successfully developed, and those commercially interested in providing organs for xenotransplantation have bred many generations of immunologically humanised pigs. But even this first stage of the process induces some ethical qualms. The genetic modification of any animal is a serious business. Although it is now widespread in agriculture, there are questions to be asked about the ethical justification for it, and how far such interference with 'natural' life forms might properly be taken. These are matters to which I shall be returning in Chapter 5.

My immediate concern is with the problem of what should happen to humanised pigs when they are no longer needed. If the breeding programme is to be maintained in order to produce a supply of young pigs for experimental purposes, the vast majority of those bred have to be killed and destroyed. They are not allowed to pass into the food chain, though they are to all intents and purposes perfectly normal pigs, indistinguishable from others except in the highly specialised context of this particular immunological reaction. The result is that many thousands of pigs have lived wasted lives and died wasted deaths. There is a minuscule possibility that the genetic modification might cause adverse effects if eaten, but the overwhelming reason why they are excluded from the food chain is the yuk factor. What would the public reaction be to the possibility of eating humanised pork? Leave aside the fact that modern pigs are the end product of centuries of selective breeding. Emotion would be likely to centre on the difference between pigs as nature intended them, and what might be felt as an abuse of the natural order of things, the dangerous crossing of a species barrier, even if only to the extent of a single gene. The fact that we already share most of our genes with pigs would probably not alleviate public concern. The whole scenario was nicely represented in a newspaper cartoon depicting a white-coated scientist saying to an apprehensive pig, 'We are moving you from research to catering.'

The other aspect of the yuk response is the reverse of this – not a reaction to humanised pigs but to porcinised humans. Xenotransplantation, whether of cells or whole organs, inevitably leads to a phenomenon known as chimerism. Individual cells from the transplant detach themselves, enter the blood stream of the human host, and are likely to end up in every organ of the body, thus becoming a permanent part of that person's physical make-up. The word 'chimerism' comes from chimera, the mythical monster made up of parts from several different animal species. Opponents of xenotransplantation make much of the idea, and cartoonists have had fun drawing pictures of people with pig's snouts and pricked-up ears. There is, of course, a medically serious side to chimerism, in that the circulating foreign cells might carry, and possibly transmit, infection. But there is also a deep, if irrational, fear that chimerism in some sense threatens human identity. Are we still truly human if parts of our body have been derived directly from a pig? It is the same fear which in the nineteenth century fuelled vigorous opposition to vaccination, on the grounds that 'innoculation with fluid from cows would result in the "animalisation" of human beings'.[22] There are reports of patients receiving human transplants, who have been disturbed by thoughts of the person whose organ they now possess. How would they feel with a pig's heart? Possible psychological reactions have been seriously discussed, but the brutal answer is that most people would almost certainly prefer to suffer minor psychological disturbance than be dead.

I have called such fears irrational because there is no scientific evidence that animal cells in a human body make the slightest difference to that person's humanity, any more than artificial limbs somehow render a person less than fully human. But the fear can feed on a philosophical question lurking in the background. How far can you go? How many organs can be replaced before a person's identity is threatened? What about a face transplant, for instance? And if the techniques for implanting foetal nerve cells in the brain to counter various degenerative conditions were to be greatly expanded, how much new brain tissue could one receive while still remaining the same person? No attempt to be clearer about what we mean by 'human nature' will by itself give us a final answer to such questions. Nevertheless it is worth trying to discern whether there are indeed given elements in human nature, and natural limits to what human beings should do and be, even if only as a safeguard against muddled thinking.

More general questions about how we are to recognise and respond to the givenness of nature in general become increasingly urgent as our powers to override it seem set to increase beyond our ability to assimilate the changes. Current controversies over GM foods, for instance, are only the tip of a very large iceberg. The question whether Mother Nature might take her revenge on those who trifle with her, is not as fanciful as it might seem.

These and other questions will be the subject of future chapters. But preceding them, in the next chapter, is the larger question raised by the concept of nature as everything there is. Is there a given reality, labelled 'nature', which is somehow analysable by beings which form part of it? Words do not necessarily correspond to things. Whether philosophical naturalism by itself is adequate to account for the world as we actually experience it, is inseparable from questions about how far our concept of nature is itself a social construct. So what is this givenness we seem to encounter? And does a proper insight into the givenness of things require that our description of it as 'given' should be more than just a metaphor? All these questions, and many more, are reasons why an exploration of the concept of nature is worth undertaking. But for me, as I suspect it was for the late Lord Gifford, the final question, whether givenness implies a giver, is the most significant of all.

Maybe I'm getting old but this is very complex.

TWO

STUDYING NATURE

Some concepts have imperialistic tendencies. They colonise areas where they did not orginally belong. 'Information' is a modern example, so much so that we now describe ourselves as living in an information society, in which information processing is one of the main activities, information one of the main products, and some people look forward to the day when human beings themselves can be understood as little more than bundles of information.

A similar escalation occurred with 'nature'. I described in the previous chapter how the third meaning of the word, 'nature' as the whole physical universe, began to predominate. When combined with the second meaning, 'nature' as a force or principle, the way was open to a thoroughgoing naturalism in which the same concept was used for both the active and the passive sides of a single reality. One could speak of Nature doing this or that, as if it were a controlling agency. But what it acted on was also Nature, the whole of the physical world. This close link between what nature is understood to be, and the laws which govern it, now lies at the heart of modern science.

Nor is it just nature in general which is thought to be reducible to laws, and ultimately, it is hoped, to sets of equations. The particular natures of things, their innate properties, nature in the first of its three senses, are also treated as reducible to the law-like behaviour of their constituent parts. Out goes Aristotle's belief that things are to be understood in terms of their purposes, to be replaced by the more Platonic notion that they can be explained by the exposure of their logical structures, the fundamental idea, nowadays generally conceived as a mathematical pattern, which makes them what they are. Within this amalgamation of the different meanings of 'nature' into a comprehensive naturalism, we find what many believe to be the essence of the scientific revolution. The totality of things must be ultimately explicable in terms of mathematical formulae which govern, not only how nature in all its parts behaves, but also fundamentally what nature is. To know the rules, therefore, is potentially to know everything, even the mind of God. Hence the much misunderstood search, popularised by Stephen Hawking, for a 'theory of everything'. One can't get more imperialistic than that.

There is a nice illustration of imperialist ambition in the title of that most prestigious scientific journal – *Nature*. The whole gamut of scientific enterprise, from natural history to the most abstruse mathematical formulation of some fundamental theory, is summed up in a single word. I suspect that this represented in some measure the sentiments of the journal's founder, of whom it was said that he 'exhibited an arrogance which would still have been offensive even had he been the Author of Nature'.

The word 'science' itself has also undergone significant changes, thereby contributing to the unspoken assumption that total knowledge was somehow within its grasp. It began as a general word for different kinds of knowledge, particularly of the more theoretical kind. But it was not until the late eighteenth century that it began to acquire a more specialised meaning, linked with experiment, empirical experience, and the methodical study of the natural world. The real revolution did not take place, however, until the mid-nineteenth century, when scientific discoveries began to have a major social impact, and when scientists themselves were struggling to professionalise their work, often against ecclesiastical vested interests. Their struggle was a sub-text of the agenda in the controversies over Darwinism, and accounted for much of T. H. Huxley's spleen against his clerical opponents.[1]

It comes as something of a shock to realise that the word 'scientist' was not coined until 1840. Nevertheless an important

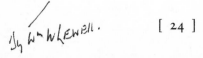
By Wm Whewell.

step in that direction had been taken in 1831 with the formation of the British Association for the Advancement of Science. Similar associations and institutes were at the same time being created all over Europe, but Britain was unlike other countries in that its Association used the word 'science' in the singular to describe its activities, whereas all others, outside the English-speaking world, used the plural 'sciences'.[2] While the difference might seem trivial, its effects have been anything but. The decision was made during a crucial period of transition from a generalised concept of natural philosophy to the designation of distinct scientific disciplines. The word 'science' was itself beginning to acquire a narrower meaning. By adopting its use in the singular the British Association in effect drew a sharp line between those disciplines which properly belonged within this newly defined realm of 'science', and those which did not. It is a distinction which had further long-term implications, in that only science, in its now restricted sense, was regarded as employing something called 'the scientific method', which in turn came to be identified by many people as providing the only rational basis for knowledge. There was some excuse for this attempted take-over bid, in that there were competing imperialisms to counter. More than forty years after the foundation of the British Association it could still be written, not entirely in jest, about the Master of Balliol, a classicist and theologian:

First come I; my name is Jowett.
There's no knowledge but I know it.
I am the Master of this college:
What I don't know isn't knowledge.[3]

The counter-claim that there is a single alternative source of knowledge – science – is not usually made in jest,[4] but has not been without its problems. It has led, for instance, to endless boundary disputes about what is properly scientific, and what is not. Are psychoanalysis and sociology sciences, for example? And does it matter if they are not? And where does the class distinction between science and lesser forms of knowledge leave theology, once 'the queen of the sciences'? I am not accusing the British Association of deliberate imperialism. Its founders were responding to the need to give scientific work a clearer image and a more professional basis. The result, though, has been to convey the impression that there is a monolithic block of knowledge, all of which fulfils certain rigorous conditions of verifiability, and thus alone has the right to make truth claims. Wise scientists know that this is not true, and are often conspicuous for their intellectual humility. The intelligentsia on the fringes of the scientific world have not always shared the same lack of presumption. Lowes Dickinson, writing in 1905, is fairly typical of what later became known as scientism: 'Religious truth, like all other truth, is attainable, if at all, only by the method of science.'[5] Similarly one of Bertrand Russell's early aims was to build philosophy itself on science.

In the rest of Europe, where the word was used in the plural, the implication was that there can be a range of sciences, appropriate to different aspects of human experience, including those human sciences like history which, by virtue of their subject matter, cannot rely on such methods as controlled and replicable experiment, or mathematical analysis. This need not make them uncritical or irrational. It simply means that their findings cannot have the same degree of exactitude, nor the same rigorousness of proof, as is possible in those sciences whose subject matter is more easily controllable, and less deeply embedded in the ambivalences of ordinary experience.

In the latter half of the nineteenth century the German philosopher Wilhelm Dilthey drew a famous distinction between the natural sciences and the human sciences, the former concerned with explanation, the latter with understanding.[6] He defined the human sciences as those studies which cannot exclude the role of the human mind in expressing intentions, generating meaning, and discerning values. Whereas the natural sciences seek for explanation in terms of objective entities and relationships, the human sciences seek for understanding through a process of interpretation within the framework of the total lived experience of being human. As Dilthey saw it, the human sciences should examine the thoughts and utterances and behaviour of human beings in such varied fields as psychology, sociology, history, art, religion and literature, without allowing individual disciplines to obscure the complexity and interconnectedness of actual human existence.

Much has happened since Dilthey's day, not least the growth of the flourishing discipline of hermeneutics, which seeks to act as a bridge, interpreting one age or culture to another. But in the English-speaking world, which still uses 'science' in the singular, the idea that there can be a wide range of sciences, each critical in its own proper way, and each with its own validity, has gained little foothold in popular perceptions of what science really is. The so-called hard sciences, those which fulfil the criteria of controlled experiment and mathematical rigour in their narrowest senses, are the stated ideal to which all other scientific enterprises should try to conform. I recall some words by a distinguished neurologist, which some fifty years ago opened my eyes to the narrowness of this ideal.

> For too many amongst us . . . the inadequate conception that 'science is measurement' and concerns itself with nothing but the metrical has become a thought-cramping obsession, and the more nearly a scientific paper approximates to a long and bloodless caravan of equations plodding across the desert pages of some journal between small and infrequent oases of words, the more quintessentially scientific it is supposed to be, though not seldom no one can tell – and few are interested to ask – whither in the kingdom of ordered knowledge the caravan is bound. Whatever may be true of the physical sciences, the day is not arrived when all the truths of medicine and biology can be reduced to this bleak residue, or when living nature can be comprehensively expressed in what fashion decrees shall be called a protocol.[7]

Modern versions of the reductionist dream, as expressed in popular culture, frequently latch onto a mistaken interpretation of the phrase 'theory of everything'.[8] What such a theory actually attempts to do is to unify some highly complex mathematical formulations in the far reaches of theoretical physics, by bringing together the two very different theories – relativity and quantum mechanics. It falls far short of the much more ambitious, and much less plausible, notion that a single theory can explain everything, and that all other sciences ought to be reducible without remainder to physics, and ultimately to mathematics.

A HIERARCHY OF SCIENCES

The subject is so crucial to questions about the meaning and scope of the concept of nature, that it is worth looking in a little more detail at how different scientific disciplines can be inter-related, and at the kind of interchanges which can take place between them. The biologist E. O. Wilson at one time elaborated a model of such interchanges, commonly known as the sandwich theory, to illustrate the simplest and most obvious kind of inter-action.[9] Imagine a hierarchy of disciplines in which each is sandwiched between one above it, which it seeks to reformulate as far as possible in terms of its own laws and concepts, and one below it, whose encroachments it seeks to resist. A typical sandwich might consist of biology, chemistry and physics. Biology, in the upper layer, tries to resist being swallowed by chemistry, in the middle, which in turn resists the complete reduction of its concepts to those of physics, at the bottom of the sandwich. The biologist is perfectly well aware that living things are composed of chemical substances, an ever-increasing number of which can now be identified and their interactions mapped. A chemical structure, the genome, provides the score for this chemical orchestra, and there are also elegant ways in which physical and even mathematical principles can be shown to underlie many biological structures and behaviours. A zebra's stripes, for instance, are neither random, nor each one individu-ally mapped. They develop as a pattern through some mathematically analysable chemical interactions of a kind found also in tigers and fish and the shells of molluscs.[10] But a zebra's behaviour cannot be reduced to chemistry or mathematics, and there is no way in which biological phenomena can be understood without introducing concepts like organisation, adaptation, and the much-derided notion of purpose – none of which belongs within chemistry itself. The distribution of stripes may be explicable in terms of mathematics and chemistry, but the origin and purpose of stripes has everything to do with biological evolution and the advantages of camouflage.

By contrast, chemistry's attempt to resist reduction to physics is more a matter of convenience than fundamental principle. In principle it ought to be possible to derive the whole of chemistry from physics. But it would be intolerably complicated to do so and, if it were actually done, chemistry would become so unwieldy as to be useless. It is enough in practice for physics to provide explanations for the most basic chemical concepts, of which valency and atomic weight were among the first examples. There is also the hybrid realm of physical chemistry. Chemistry, in short, can make considerable territorial gains, but not a complete take-over bid, within the realm of biology, and is itself vulnerable in principle, though not in practice, to assimilation by physics. By contrast neither chemistry nor biology can make any direct contribution to physics and mathematics, other than by alerting them to new problems requiring solution. Chaos and complexity theories, for example, have arisen out of this kind of interaction.[11] Indeed most of the striking scientific advances more often than not take place on the frontiers between established disciplines.

The pattern of potential encroachments from below means that the human sciences, which are near the top of the multi-layered sandwich, as dealing with more complex and highly differentiated subject matter, tend to receive more interpretative insights, which may be constructive or destructive, from the lower, seemingly more fundamental, disciplines than they can contribute to them in return. Theology, for example, has gained immeasurably from, and also in some respects been radically changed by, a better understanding of the physical universe as disclosed by the natural sciences. But it has had to defend itself, among many other things, from assumptions about an all-embracing physical determinism, which is more or less taken for granted as belonging to a proper scientific methodology. The conflict is endemic because the scientific search for efficient causes necessarily presupposes determinism. This presupposition, however, is itself vulnerable to philosophical questioning about how causality can actually be proved, and about the role of the human mind in enabling us to recognise causal connections. Since the days of Hume and Kant these have been familiar philosophical problems,[12] but to go further into them would take me too far from my main theme. The usual theological riposte to the kind of determinism which would eliminate human free will, treads simpler ground by appealing to the ordinary experience of human life. Actually to believe that all one's thoughts and actions were predetermined would cut the nerve of moral effort. Paradoxically it would also be destructive of critical and creative initiatives, not least those daring new thoughts which led philosophers to ponder such matters as causality in the first place. In face of this and other kinds of attack from below, theology's repeated defence is to point to the primary awareness of being responsible and creative human beings. It resists the relegation of this awareness to a less significant status and role, on the grounds that it cannot be over-ridden by theoretical assumptions derived from the methodology of the natural sciences, which are themselves one of its products.

Theology's own contribution to the natural sciences has often been to remind them of this wider, more value-orientated context in which their work is done. In so doing it also seeks to provide a rationale for the unity and intelligibility of the natural world.

Sociology occupies a rather ambivalent position in the hierarchy, and is equally adept at seeking to colonise both theology and the natural sciences, on the grounds that they are social constructions.

The general picture is that the traffic downwards, say from a human science to a physical one, consists in showing that the latter's concepts are too narrow to contain all that the more human science needs to take account of. New properties, needing new forms of conceptual understanding, emerge at successive levels, and cannot be reduced to what, in a physical sense, may be more fundamental categories. The traffic upwards may in turn shed new light on higher level phenomena, by revealing how some complex processes may have quite simple explanations. The zebra's stripes, for instance, are not a miracle of planning; they merely follow a formula. In short, the sandwich model of a hierarchy of interrelated sciences, studying different subject matters and using different methods and terminologies, offers a subtle and dynamic understanding of what the sciences are and how they work, and provides a rich many-levelled concept of nature, which wears different faces dependent on the different questions put to it. The model, in other words, is *prima facie* evidence that the concept of nature as studied by science needs much more careful articulation than it usually receives, as also does the concept of science itself. But, like all such models, it is an over-simplification.

The actual interrelationships and cross-overs between the different scientific disciplines are much more complex than up and down movement through a series of layers might suggest. Nevertheless the assumption that science, as it were, bottoms out in physics is deeply entrenched. It is with this assumption in mind that I now return to some of the most fundamental physical concepts themselves, and ask on what it is that, in the end, the whole edifice of the scientific knowledge of nature purports to be resting.

RATIONAL EXPLANATION

Einstein, who more than anyone else in the last century changed our understanding of the ultimate structure of the physical world, never did a single laboratory experiment, except presumably as a student. He did, of course, use experimental results obtained by others, but his great achievements were in the realm of scientific imagination, in thinking the hitherto unthinkable and expressing it in mathematical form. It was said of him that 'He believed that theories into which facts were later seen to fit were more likely to stand the test of time than theories constructed entirely from experimental evidence.'[13] He had an extraordinary feel for the way physics ought to be, and for the ability of pure thought to grasp reality, almost as if he were in the world of the ancient Greeks who had shared the same dream. And he had acquired the mathematical skills which enabled such thoughts to take a precise and calculable form.

In the end, as he well recognised, theories have to be tested by experience, but for a long time the tests of his own theories were minimal, and the results not entirely conclusive. Nor have they remained unchallenged. Recent speculations that the velocity of light might not have been constant during the history of the universe would, if confirmed, destroy the central assumption on which relativity is based.[14] But when the two theories of relativity were first published it was the cogency of their mathematics, and their ability to explain what had hitherto been physical anomalies, which gave them their persuasive power. The fact that Einstein went on to squander the rest of his life in trying to find a mathematical reconciliation between relativity and quantum mechanics, is striking evidence of his unyielding belief that mathematics held the ultimate clue to nature. It was typical of him that he should even be instinctively uncomfortable with the idea that there are fundamental constants in nature, such as the velocity of light itself, and he would no doubt have wanted to look beyond the six independent numbers which the present Astronomer Royal believes are both necessary and sufficient to explain why the universe is as it is.[15] Natural constants of this latter kind appear to be simply given, and it has not been possible to derive them from existing theories, other than by the extravagant postulate of an infinity of universes in which all possible constants are represented. Einstein complained about the very existence of such irreducible factors:

A theory which in its fundamental equations explicitly contains a constant would have to be somehow constructed of bits and pieces which are logically independent of each other; but I am confident that this world is not such that so ugly a construction is needed for its theoretical comprehension.[16]

But why should anybody expect mathematics to tell us everything? Why should it loom so large in the physicist's understanding of nature? It is part of the belief that physical reality fulfils the requirements of logic. That is an idea which ought at first sight to be congenial to theologians, as it was to the Greeks. Our God is a God of order. But in practice too rigorous an application of what is currently accepted as logic can lead, and has led, to terrible mistakes. One of the most persistent ideas in the history of Western thought, from Plato to the beginning of the nineteenth century, was that nature ought to be regarded as a 'great chain of being'.[17] It was assumed that in a rational world created by God as an expression of his goodness, all possible forms of the good would need to be made actual. The hallmark of creation, in other words, was fullness, plenitude. Nature was envisaged as a continuum, stretching from the stars to the tiniest creature, in which every logically possible form of being was represented. Things existed because it was logically necessary for them to exist, so that they could fill the place allotted to them within the created order. There was even dispute about whether separate species existed, or whether there was complete unbroken gradation from one living thing to another, with species representing only artificial distinctions, a matter of language rather than of 'unmovable boundaries set by nature'.[18] Locke, for instance, was inclined to the view that the distinctions between species were only a matter of definition – a view which interestingly enough is beginning to creep back in our own day. Thus the search for 'missing links', which nowadays we associate with Darwinism, was not at first an evolutionary quest at all. It rested on the assumption that the gaps in natural history must be closed because, as Leibnitz put it, 'God makes the greatest number of things that he can.'[19]

The trouble with this idea of plenitude was that it became increasingly difficult to square with actual experience. Despite the valid sense in which evolution can be described as an exploration of all possible ways of being alive, natural selection remains a haphazard contingent process, not a necessary one, and there is no guarantee that, in a world of time and chance, all that might be will be. To start with a supposed theoretical necessity, and to allow it to shape the expectations with which nature was studied, was a recipe for eventual disillusionment. Yet it went on for centuries, and not least during the Age of Reason. It leaves us with the question of how far we in our day are justified in subscribing to theoretical formulations about the ultimate nature of things, expressed in mathematics so complex that few people in the world can understand it. Are we in danger of falling into the same trap?

Some years ago I received a long series of letters from a retired professor of physics who believed passionately that Einstein was wrong about relativity, and that the world was in danger if it was so foolish as to persist in developing techniques which depended on his being right. Why he felt an archbishop might help him was never clear to me, but it was obvious that he had been ostracised by all his scientific colleagues, even though most of them could not provide a satisfactory answer to the logical problem about time travel which was perplexing him.[20]

His question was this. 'According to the special theory of relativity, two similar clocks, A and B, which are in uniform relative motion and in which no other differences exist of which the theory takes any account, work at different rates. The situation is therefore entirely symmetrical, from which it follows that if A works faster than B, B must work faster than A. Since this is impossible, the theory must be false.'

This looks like a straightforward logical argument, and it was obvious that a great many of the distinguished scientists to whom it was sent were nonplussed by it. Nevertheless they took Einstein on trust, and relied on their more mathematical colleagues to demonstrate a different kind of logic which is beyond the grasp of most ordinary mortals. The controversy is now forgotten and my correspondent is dead, but I mention the incident to illustrate how far modern physics has taken us into a realm where ordinary perceptions of what is logical fail us, where it is no longer possible to picture the reality we are dealing with, and where theoretical physicists are entirely dependent on highly sophisticated mathematical tools and abstract concepts to make what sense they can of the empirical data.

THE KEY ROLE OF MATHEMATICS

Perhaps my question about why ultimate explanations are to be sought in mathematics needs to be reshaped. How is it that this particular form of abstract thinking has been so successful in matching the results of experiment? Part of the reason must be that mathematical techniques were developed specifically in order to tackle the precise and complex calculations scientists needed to make. There is an element of circularity here. Newton, for instance, developed a form of calculus when he was in his early twenties in order to describe the orbit of the moon. Other seventeenth century scientists were doing the same in trying to tackle various mechanical problems. Einstein, by contrast, took his mathematics off the peg. It just so happened that, some forty years before he needed it, the kind of geometry required by the General Theory of Relativity had been devised as a purely theoretical exercise by a young German mathematician, Georg Riemann, who had been exploring the geometry of curved surfaces. But in the second half of Einstein's life, when he was obsessed with repeated attempts to unify physics by bringing together relativity and quantum mechanics, the mathematics was not there. Nor could he invent it.

He was not alone in having come to believe that one should look to mathematics to supply answers to the most fundamental questions about the nature of physical reality. Sir Arthur Eddington, the most famous astrophysicist of his day, spent years trying to derive the basic physical constants from abstract theory by performing what many of his colleagues dismissed as 'arithmetical gymnastics'.[21] He was duly ridiculed for it. Yet both men in their way were feeling back to the ancient Greek view of a world based on rational necessity. It was as if mathematics were felt somehow to exist independently of the minds of those who construct theories. From this perspective mathematical truths are simply there, waiting to be discovered rather than invented, because they are believed ultimately to represent the way things are.

Invented or discovered? A tool devised to fit the circumstances of the world as perceived by physicists, or the discovery of sets of logical relationships which in some sense really exist? The debate has continued, and the answer seems to be – a bit of both. From a biological perspective one of the oddities in the story of the triumph of mathematics is that the logical operations of the human mind seem so well adapted to deal with complexities which were not even remotely in view during the hundreds of thousands of years in which our mental capacities were evolving. Perhaps the answer is that the capacity to use highly abstract concepts in making sense of experience developed hand in hand with the need to do so. Each may have prompted and promoted the other. Sometimes they have been out of step, as when speculative theories have raced ahead of empirical discovery, or when discoveries have been missed because their implications were too complex to handle.

How did it all begin? There is evidence that the practice of counting can precede the concept of number. A West African people, for instance, count by using different body parts, just as young children use fingers. They also use shortcuts, making two hands the equivalent of ten fingers without counting the fingers individually. But the whole process appears to be an entirely physical operation, unrelated to the patterns of thought which, among numerate people, can be substituted for the actual use of fingers and hands.[22] To have the concept of number requires an ability to abstract and universalise, capacities which there may have been no need to develop in isolated, non-literate cultures, where all measurements were approximate, and only the simplest business transactions took place. Forms of social life are perfectly possible, in which actions and stories convey all that needs to be communicated.

In Chinese imperial culture there was a form of counting which entailed putting rods into boxes, another primarily physical action, but one with much greater potential for being conceptualised. In fact as early as the thirteenth century B.C., there are descriptions of boxes arranged in groups of ten, with different positions of the groups representing different powers of ten – compelling evidence that the Chinese already used quite a sophisticated decimal system. The system could also allow for some boxes to be empty, thus implicitly suggesting the concept of zero. The Babylonians also had a symbol signifying an empty space. There is uncertainty, though, as to whether it was the Chinese, the Indians following the Babylonian example, or even the Indochinese, who actually invented the concept of zero as a number, one of the crucial insights opening the way to modern mathematics.[23] But there is no doubt that the Chinese made astonishing mathematical advances, many of which undergirded their equally remarkable technology. However, for reasons which may have had something to do with their excessively bureaucratic culture, they failed to exploit these advances as fully as they might have done in the construction of scientific theory. The result was that the science and the technology gradually faded away and were forgotten, until unearthed in the twentieth century by the monumental work of Joseph Needham.[24] It was in the West, partly with Arab help, that the application of mathematics to the systematic study of nature was to generate theoretical foundations for science which had previously been lacking.

The Pythagorean philosophers had been able to take the first tentative steps towards a scientific approach to the natural world because, as mentioned in the previous chapter, they had discovered a structural principle in music that every string player has to learn – number determines the quality of sound. As the name Pythagoras reminds us, they were renowned for their geometry, but they could not pursue their arithmetical insights much further. Geometry is possible without the concept of zero, but arithmetic soon runs into insoluble contradictions. It also quickly becomes clear that simple numerical ratios and geometrical forms are not in themselves adequate to account for the actual complexity of the world. Nor, even in the realm of sound, is mathematics of much help in distinguishing between music and noise, not least because there is an inevitably subjective element in the distinction. Furthermore, numbers in classical Greece and Rome were extremely difficult to handle as long as each number was separately represented by a letter of the alphabet. Anyone who has tried to do long division using Roman numerals will know the frustrations. And the Greek system was even worse. Complicated calculations only became possible when the Arabs introduced Europe to our present system of writing numerals, according to which zero is a number and the size of any number depends on the position of its various numerals. Thus one can stand for ten, a hundred, or a thousand, and so on, depending on what follows it. This invention, or rather reinvention, of a notation whereby number depends on position, two thousand years after the Chinese had done the same thing with their boxes, was one of the crucial turning points in the invention of the modern world. It meant that numbers could at last be manipulated in ways which began to match the actual complexity of experience.

In the absence of an effective numerical system the ancients focused mainly on geometry. It seems likely that the abstract concept of 'form' grew from this concentration on geometrical shape, and so gradually became for Aristotle the main word for describing the nature of things. We thus reach the curious paradox that though he wrote about the philosophy of numbers, he did not actually use them as a basis for explanation. It was only with Galileo some 2000 years later that mathematics began to occupy its key role in physics, and so started the process of rapid mutual growth which has now put them both beyond the reach of all but a select few. But even he was still heavily dependent on geometry. 'Philosophy,' he wrote

> is written in that vast book which stands ever open before our eyes, I mean the universe; but it cannot be read until we have learnt the language and become familiar with the characters in which it is written. It is written in mathematical language, and the letters are triangles, circles and other geometrical figures, without which means it is humanly impossible to comprehend a single word.[25]

In the years which followed, mathematics evolved to match the emerging complexity of nature. It has also transcended nature in its ability to bring logic and order at a fundamental level, not only to our understanding of the physical universe, but to the exploration of possible worlds, and even to the notion of an infinity of universes. Has this been a story of discovery or invention? The difference may seem hardly to matter, in that the confidence to transcend hands-on experience has in practice arisen out of scientific successes on a much more mundane level. Mathematics has been a highly successful instrument for making and manipulating significant measurements on earth, because this is what numbers were invented to do. The application of it to the exploration of the stars, to the intimate probing of the structure of matter itself, and even to the statistical analysis of human behaviour, has at every stage seemed like a reasonable extrapolation of insights and techniques which have been shown to work. But the more comprehensive its sway, and the more complex the abstractions to which it leads us, the sharper the questions become as to whether this is all just a wonderful human invention, or whether mathematics itself somehow discloses to us the true nature of reality.[26]

Before considering the further implications of this question, it will be useful to look more closely at the kind of explanations of the physical world, which mathematics has made possible.

AN INTELLIGIBLE UNIVERSE

The scientific study of nature has to a large extent relied on the exploitation of a simple principle which is common both to mathematics and to those natural sciences which most depend on it. It is the principle that a comparatively small number of basic constituents can in combination give rise to an enormous variety of possible outcomes.[27] Twenty-six letters of the alphabet are more than enough for all the books which will ever be written. Start with the concept of number and a few logical rules, and the whole of mathematics can unfold itself. Start with a few basic particles, nowadays further reduced in number by being defined in terms of a series of symmetrical relationships, and in theory it ought to be possible to explain the entire physical universe. We now know that all life depends on a genetic code made by different arrangements of only four amino acids. The greatest compression of all occurs in information technology, which has reached the theoretical limit. All information can be coded in terms of just two variables, 0 or 1, open or closed, yes or no.

Whether such compressed information is adequate to convey all that human beings can know, is a different question, to which I shall be returning later. Aristotle was clear that it could not, which is why he refused to accept the reductionism entailed in Democritus's atomic theory, and in consequence had to postulate a particular form determining the nature of each class of object he studied. As he saw it, reality in botany and biology subsisted in actual plants and animals, not in intellectual abstractions. Though based on a sound instinct, at the time this proved to be a false choice. Democritus had in principle grasped the idea that limitless differences could be explained in terms of various combinations of a limited number of fixed entities, whereas Aristotle's concentration on organic models blocked the way to further scientific progress. Darwin, by contrast, managed to bring coherence to biology, grappling with the amazing diversity of living things, through an insight which could be stated in a single sentence.

The rules by which complex forms can be generated may differ in kind. If they follow a simple linear pattern, as when B invariably follows A and is itself always followed by C, then no matter how complex the outcome, this can, like the movements of the planets, be predicted provided that the formula is known. But when the rules do not follow a linear pattern, when C following on from A and B also has repercussions on A, then things are not so easy, and reliable prediction may be impossible. Non-linear equations may have multiple solutions. What this means in practice is that when the interactions between the different parts of a system are dependent on one another, the outcome can be extremely sensitive to small changes in the initial conditions. This is the best-known implication of what is now called Chaos Theory, and it has become apparent that the world is full of such systems, the weather being a prime example.[28] Though the powers of prediction in such systems are always likely to be limited, this does not mean that what happens in them is indeterminate. Even the unpredictable should in principle be traceable back after the event to identifiable causes, so the belief that it is possible to compress immense complexity into a few basic rules, is not undermined by events which follow a non-linear pattern. Indeed it is this belief in the ultimate reducibility of even the most complex phenomena to an ordered mathematical pattern, which has been the inspiration for research in fields which at first sight seemed unpromising. But, as I have argued earlier, with reference to the sandwich model, the strict reductionist approach is not the only, and not always the most appropriate, way of understanding what is going on. Nor does it follow from the successes of reductionist science that the rules all have to be mathematical, as Darwin himself demonstrated. But it is worth noting how confidence in Darwinism greatly increased as, in the 1930s, evolutionary theory was given a statistical basis.[29]

These caveats apart, the general picture of the physical world which has gained credence in our day is that it is composed of a relatively small number of discrete constituents, whose behaviour can be represented by mathematical equations. Every electron can be treated as being identical with every other electron, every neutron identical with every other neutron, and so on down the scale. The fact that, according to quantum theory, even energy itself comes in discrete packets, provides a reason why the properties of atoms are not infinitely variable. Their components can only exist in a limited number of states. If this were not so, science would be impossible because there would be no fixed conceptual base on which to build. As it is, physics can rest on the belief that the fundamental constituents of matter are not infinitely variable, even though nature at this quantum level is not picturable by us, and though mathematically comprehensible, seems to defy ordinary logic. In trying to picture it we run into the same problem as that faced by the earliest Greek philosophers. The ultimate stuff of reality cannot be like any one part of our ordinary experience – air or fire or water or any other picturable phenomenon, as was once supposed – or we would be plunged into a vicious circle of explanations, all of them depending on each other.

Nevertheless, despite the perplexities about ultimate reality, a system of this kind in which a small range of identical but numerous components interact according to fixed rules, is in principle intelligible to us, even though it may not be fully describable, nor its future state fully predictable. It is intelligible, because it allows us to trace fundamental connections between definable events, and thus to understand mathematically how and why things happen; this is the task of the physical sciences. I have been concerned to make the point, though, that the natural world of ordinary experience is not fully describable in these abstract terms. The emergence of new properties at different levels of complexity shows the need for an understanding of each level in terms appropriate to it, and this is why there has to be a hierarchy of sciences. Events at every level are less than fully predictable because of the complexity of the interactions. But there is the further reason, familiar in quantum theory, that to observe the fundamental operations of nature is also to change them. In trying to elucidate nature, we cannot in the end leave ourselves as observers out of the equation. The natural world contains minds which have developed hitherto undreamt-of mathematical powers whereby to compress huge quantities of data into formulae. But in doing so we also become aware of limits to our understanding, some of which are inherent in the basic constituents of nature itself, and some of which are inherent in our own role in studying it.

It is thus not only in quantum theory that we meet, as it were, a barrier of uncertainty and indescribability. At other levels too in the scientific hierarchy there are limitations on what can be known. In biology, for instance, it is not possible to overcome individual unpredictability. Populations of animals can be treated statistically with a fair degree of precision. But individuals cannot be known thoroughly enough for any observer to be certain about their exact behaviour. If they were to be studied with the necessary thoroughness, that in itself would be likely to change what they did. These uncertainties created by the role of the observer are even more evident in a subject like history. The writing of history is a matter of selection and construction; selection because the data are potentially inexhaustible, and construction because to make sense of them the historian has to have some preliminary aims and organising concepts. As for theology, it has to start with the daunting recognition that its subject matter ultimately surpasses all our human powers of knowing. All knowledge of God is to some extent constructed, conditioned knowledge; constructed in that to communicate at all about God has required the development of a language of symbols, metaphors and analogies, and conditioned because this process of forging an appropriate language can only take place within particular historical circumstances, and be embodied in particular stories and statements. Nevertheless the theologian, while admitting the difficulties, may validly ask whether any other form of knowledge entirely escapes similar constraints.

With this thought in mind we need to look again at the seemingly unanswerable questions about the nature of mathematics itself.

LIMITS OF INTELLIGIBILITY

Earlier when asking whether mathematics is an invention or a discovery, I suggested that it might be a bit of both. The answer makes a difference to our understanding of nature because, if the deep structure of things is only comprehensible in mathematical terms, we need to know whether, and to what degree, our understanding has been achieved through concepts we have ourselves invented and imposed on nature. This is not quite the Kantian question about knowledge, but is related to it. Kant believed that mathematics could be synthesised by rational thought on the basis of intuitions about quantity (arithmetic) and space (geometry). These intuitions, however, soon ran into trouble, and only a few decades were to pass before geometers were beginning to make the intuition of space look decidedly arbitrary. Early in the nineteenth century the first explorations of the possibility of non-Euclidian geometry demonstrated that different concepts of space were conceivable. In the following century Einstein completed the process of destroying Kant's intuition with his non-Euclidian and highly counter-intuitive concept of what spatial reality is like.

The belief that arithmetic could be synthesised from a bare intuition of quantity fared no better. Bertrand Russell was responsible for the most famous and strenuous effort to go beyond Kant by attempting to derive mathematics entirely from logic.[30] It failed and, as was seen later, necessarily failed, when it was demonstrated by Gödel's famous incompleteness theorem that there can be no consistent formal system in which every mathematical truth is provable.[31]

If then pure logic cannot give us mathematics, what can? The suggestion that in some Platonic sense mathematical reality does not need to be grounded in our own powers of deduction, but exists apart from our knowledge of it, has its attractions, not least to those who would locate it somehow in the mind of God. Certainly there are features of mathematics which support the view that it grasps hold of something out there waiting to be discovered.[32] The beauty of much of it, the endless fascination of such ineluctable facts as the distribution and properties of prime numbers, and the intuitive grasp by great mathematicians of theorems which cannot at the time be proved, point to a kind of reality independent of us. Public interest in the recent proof of Fermat's Last Theorem, for instance, after 250 years of trying, has focused on the mystery of how Fermat could have claimed a discovery, when the actual demonstration of it had to make use of methods which could not possibly have been available to him at the time.[33] Did he just make a lucky guess? Or did he have the kind of feel for mathematical reality that Einstein had for physics?

It is clear, too, from what I have said earlier about counting, that mathematics has empirical origins, and its symbiotic relationship with modern science has tended to maintain this sense of rootedness in reality. There are difficulties, though, when both of them transcend the boundaries of what the human mind can envisage. If, as is now claimed, theories about the ultimate constitution of matter require a mathematics capable of handling anything between six and 25 dimensions of space, it stretches credibility to suppose that appropriate mathematical constructions of this inconceivable complexity were somehow pre-existent, simply waiting to be discovered.[34] It is equally hard to know what existence in 25 dimensions could possibly mean outside the mathematical clothes in which the idea has been dressed. Multiple dimensions, alongside many other esoteric mathematical constructions, look much more like convenient fictions, invented for particular purposes, than like pre-existing truths written somehow into the constitution of the universe. It may transpire that these hugely complex mathematical constructions, which at present seem to represent the furthest that theoretical physicists can take us in the attempt to grasp the ultimate secrets of nature, are no more than the products of human imagination, finely tuned to the questions physicists have chosen to ask. Or they may be claimed as real discoveries on the grounds that they represent the sort of answers which nature requires us to give. The whole subject is immensely difficult, both scientifically and philosophically. In philosophical terms it is part of the longstanding and highly nuanced controversy between realists and structuralists, and I confess to being a long way out of my depth. It is usually the case, however, that where such longstanding controversies exist, both sides are eventually found to have been expressing some part of the truth. In such a baffling context a comment by the mathematician Hans-Christian Reichel seems apposite: 'What we learn from mathematics is just as unanswerable as "What do we learn from Tolstoy's *War and Peace?*" '[35]

War and Peace is a work of fiction, a marvellous creation of the human mind. It is also rooted in real events, and would have lost a major part of its significance had it been set in Ruritania rather than in Russia. Like all great works of art it communicates truthfully on a variety of different levels, but it can only do so by the personal involvement of the reader in the story. What we learn from it depends on who we are, and what we ask of it. The suggestion that this might also be the case in the scientific study of nature is likely to meet with resistance from most scientists. Is it not one of the distinguishing marks of good science that the scientist should be invisible, an austerely objective operator, in principle replaceable by any other operator with similar skills? The repellently detached style in which scientific papers are usually written, witnesses to this distancing of the person from the results of their research, thus hiding the emotional reality and general messiness of actual scientific thinking and experimentation. A caravan of equations plodding across an arid desert has no need to display a human face. A high level of abstraction may be a mark of scientific excellence, but it leaves out half the picture. It is in highlighting the other half, the personal and social factors, that sociologists of science have brought a different perspective to bear on scientific work, disclosing insights which have not been wholly welcomed within the scientific community.

A SOCIOLOGICAL PERSPECTIVE

The suggestion that research in the natural sciences may not be as objective, rational, and straightforwardly descriptive of reality as it claims to be, frequently meets with outright rejection.[36] The sociologist would claim in reply to be doing no more than subjecting the processes and circumstances of scientific work itself to the same kinds of observation, theorising, and critical scrutiny, which have been responsible for the stunning success of the natural sciences in the past three or four centuries. The subject matter may be more difficult, and the concepts less sharply defined, but the need for criticism is no less great.

It is this sort of criticism – whether by others or better still by scientists themselves – focused on the human context of research, which may help to throw light on some of the problems at which I have been hinting. In particular there is the notion of fundamental explanation, in which there seems to be an uncomfortable element of circularity. We think we know what rationality is on the basis of our publicly shared experience of the ordinary world. Mathematics, which is at least in some respects a human construction, pushes rationality to extreme limits in trying to lay bare the fundamental structure of nature, even when its conclusions are unpicturable and seem to defy the logic of the ordinary world on which its analysis has been based. Knowing that we ourselves are part of nature, with minds which have evolved for quite other purposes than pursuing abstract logic, how can we be confident in the powers of reason as we approach these seemingly illogical limits? Furthermore our concepts of what is rational, rooted in ordinary experience, have also been socially conditioned. We are therefore predisposed to accept the practical results of science because they confirm our experience of the kind of world we have now come to expect. But who are 'we' who do these things and adopt these attitudes? We are members of a particular culture which, over many centuries, has learnt to rely on scientific knowledge as the most effective basis for the understanding and successful manipulation of the natural world. Science is trusted because it works, and because it can in the long run create consensus. Though intrinsically its successes may seem to depend on supposedly crucial experiments, in practice it depends on the general acceptance of its results by those fellow-specialists who understand them. In fact it is an essentially social activity.

As such it falls within the scope of sociology, as well as exemplifying one of the defining characteristics of post-modern culture, namely an awareness of the conditioned nature of all truth-claims. The mind which seizes on an apparently obvious connection has itelf been conditioned in what to expect. Each of us belongs to our time and place, with all the limitations that entails. In the seventeenth century, for example, explanations of natural phenomena were sought entirely in terms of mechanical causes, however unlikely the mechanism proposed, because this is what Cartesian philosophy prescribed and what educated society was led to expect. Nerves were thought to be pipes, down which liquid flowed to contract the muscles. However ridiculous the idea might seem to us now, it was a reasonable hypothesis in its own day, given the conceptual limitations of a science in which the notion of irritable tissue had not been invented, and electricity was unknown. It would be surprising if we in the twenty-first century were not blinkered by our own set of conceptual limitations. It may be that such limitations will only be exposed by the kind of cross-disciplinary discussion which enables unconscious presuppositions and cultural conditioning to be brought out into the open. Such periodic reassessments are the inevitable consequence of having acquired minds disposed to be reflexively critical, and sociology is potentially one of the useful tools for doing just this, by alerting us to the influence of our social environment.

Why then is it regarded with such suspicion? If it is true that scientists are creatures of their own time, and that scientific theories are social constructions from concepts available in a particular culture, what grounds are there for objecting? One reason is that some sociological critics of the natural sciences have tended to go so far in relativising all truth claims that the choices between them begin to look arbitrary. Thomas Kuhn's ground-breaking work on 'scientific revolutions' with its claim that there may be 'incommensurable paradigms' has helped to encourage the view that there may be no rational way of deciding between different world views.[37] This was surely not Kuhn's intention, but it has been grist to the mill for postmodernists and others, including unfortunately some religious apologists.[38] The temptation to define incompatible belief systems as 'incommensurable paradigms', and yet as all capable of being regarded as true, has all too often proved irresistible.

Sociological analysis of particular research establishments has usefully drawn attention to the significance of local factors and personalities in research priorities, styles of work, and the needs and assumptions of individual researchers.[39] It can also give substance to legitimate fears about the increasing dependence of such establishments on commercial interests, and the difficulties of adequate peer review under the conditions of commercial confidentiality. It has proved easy, however, to exaggerate the importance of such insights by inflating them into the much more dubious claim that science is essentially local, and locally conditioned, and only becomes universal by negotiation with the scientific community as a whole.

In both examples the identification of a strong element of social construction within scientific work is frequently dismissed by natural scientists as a threat to what they conceive their work to be really about. But this is to disregard some useful insights into the necessarily conditioned character of all human knowledge, by confusing them with judgements about bias and limitations in scientific method itself. As the author of a recent study of stages in the development of thinking has put it:

> The long history of philosophical attempts to figure out what good science should be, turned out to be a history of increasing awareness of the subjective element in science. Where science long has tried to pin down reality as the objective 'known', the philosophy of science has shown the presence of the subjective 'knower' more and more clearly in all supposedly objective knowledge. Historians of science have joined in this exposé. So have those doing sociology of knowledge. Unfortunately, philosophers, historians, and sociologists have sometimes concluded that because science is a human construction, it cannot have universal validity and reliability.[40]

But how, when the subjective element is properly recognised, are universal validity and reliability to be defended, except on the basis I have already described? The point is that in practice scientific methods work. It is possible in fact to give a Darwinian account of science in which those theories survive, which provide the best explanations and the best predictive success.[41] Just as certain organisms succeed because they are adapted to their environment, so certain theories succeed because they make sense of some aspect of reality, and are fruitful in breeding further discoveries. A potential difficulty with this analogy is that organisms do not adapt to the environment as a whole, but to some niche within it where they are best at doing their own thing.[42]

But even this, as I have already indicated, is not unlike what actually happens in scientific laboratories, where much of what goes on is local, particular, adjusted to a special set of circumstances, and driven by the needs and assumptions of those doing the research. The evolutionary model has a further refinement, in that living organisms are not passive players within their competitive world. They are active participants trying to make the best of it on the basis of their own special characteristics. Nor, likewise, are scientific theories passive receptacles into which observations are collected and then ordered. Good science starts with theories and tests them against observations, sometimes finding them strengthened in the process, sometimes in need of adaptation, and sometimes destroyed. In a word, scientific research is theory-laden, in the sense that theory comes first, before the experiments designed to test it.

Generalising this point to refer to the scientific enterprise as a whole, it is possible to envisage a kind of virtuous circle in which, despite initial misconceptions, the understanding of nature is progressively refined through the testing and revision of theoretical constructions, until they fit more and more closely the reality of what is actually observed. However, uncritical reliance on supposedly established theoretical constructions, entails the alternative possibility that the virtuous circle whereby reality is disclosed, may turn out to be not so virtuous after all. Furthermore while most scientists are prepared to recognise that all research is theory-laden, there is much greater reluctance to accept that theory-ladenness might apply to the scientific enterprise as a whole.

Blindness to these possibilities may have the effect of bracketing out aspects of reality which do not fit the preconceptions of a scientific culture. It may promote a concept of rationality which is not adequate to the full range of human experience. This has certainly happened in the past, as in my previous example of the seventeenth-century attempt to explain the action of nerves in purely mechanical terms. Similarly, current attempts to understand consciousness in terms of information theory may shed some light on the way we think, but at the cost of setting on one side whatever it is we mean by subjective experience. Information theory itself has not until very recently been seen as relevant to the mysterious world of quantum phenomena, yet the simple idea that nature only answers the questions we ask it, and in the form we ask them, may go a long way towards explaining some of the oddities at this quantum level.[43] I shall be returning in the final chapter to the idea that a whole dimension of our human environment and experience has been bracketed out by the assumption that nature, as currently understood, is all there is.

CONCLUSION

I have been arguing in this chapter that the study of nature in its wholeness requires a range of disciplines, and different levels of understanding. All explanations at whatever level, to a greater or lesser degree entail some element of human construction, and all confront us with an element of givenness, against which our ideas about reality have to be measured. We can look for ultimate reality in the fine structure of matter but the mathematics which gives us our only means of understanding it has itself an ambivalent status as both invented and discovered. Or we can look for reality, as Aristotle did, in the world as actually experienced. Reality, from this perspective, is what confronts us here and now, organisms not atoms, which is why our probing of other levels of understanding should not be allowed to detract from the wholeness of lived experience.

Between these extremes there is plenty of room for discussion, and some appreciation of the many dimensions of the concept of nature may be a good place to start. As we shall see in subsequent chapters, the classic dualism between nature and culture may have to be redefined. It may have to be conceded that a God-like perspective on the natural world is not available to us, precisely because we are not gods. Indeed it may be that theology's main contribution to the discussion is to go on offering reminders of that fundamental truth.

THREE

RESPECTING NATURE

Towards the end of 1999 I was lucky enough to encounter a herd of quaggas. They were grazing on scrubland in the southern part of the Great Karoo in South Africa. Officially quaggas have been extinct since the 1880s. Enormous herds of them used to roam over the central plains of Africa, but they were hunted mercilessly by colonial sportsmen, until all that remained were a few stuffed specimens in European natural history museums. Quaggas were related to zebras but had distinctive markings, with black stripes only at the front, unstriped chocolate coloured coats at the rear, and white underbellies. Some zebras still have a few quagga-like features, and over more than a decade these have been selectively bred to enhance residual quagga-like genes, with the result that the new herd are beginning to look astonishingly like their stuffed ancestors.

But are they really quaggas? And what do we mean by a real quagga anyway? Does a species have to enjoy a direct continuity with its past in order to be a natural species, or is there no essential difference between a natural species and one which has been artificially raised from the dead? Also, given that the process started before it was realised that there might be remnants of DNA from which they could be cloned, why would anybody want to recreate extinct animals by such a laborious and time-consuming method as selective breeding over many generations? And why is the motive likely to reflect such a very different attitude from that of the hunters who originally exterminated them?

The answer to the last two questions, of course, is that many people's perceptions of the fragility of the natural world have changed radically within the last 40 years. There is a growing consciousness of what has been lost, and might be lost in the future. But there remain large questions about what is actually meant by 'the natural world', and in what sense a reconstructed quagga might be said to belong to it. My concern in the last chapter was with the concept of nature as comprising everything, the whole physical universe including ourselves. In this chapter I shall be exploring some more restricted meanings, centred on the concept of nature as, to a greater or lesser degree, distinct from ourselves.

It is a concept beset by paradoxes. What could be more paradoxical than the attempt to restore nature, in the form of an extinct species, by means which are wholly dependent on human interference? Add to that the paradox that the area in the Great Karoo where the quaggas are being bred, is itself to a certain extent artificial. It was at one time farmland, and on conversion to a nature reserve was deliberately restocked with its original fauna and flora. Untouched nature is a rare commodity nowadays, and in most parts of the world even the designation of an area as wilderness entails prescribing artificial boundaries, and limited access. Visitors find their wilderness experience by courtesy of the government, and there are clearly different expectations of what a wilderness should be. The US Forest Service has recorded a number of complaints from visitors on the Internet, including: 'There are too many rocks in the mountains', 'Escalators would help on steep uphill sections', 'Too many bugs and leeches and spiders and spider webs. Please spray the wilderness to rid the area of these pests', and 'A small deer came into my camp and stole my bag of pickles. Is there a way I can get reimbursed?'[1]

Recent worries about what modern civilisations have done to the earth's atmosphere, and hence in all probability to the weather, take us to the heart of the paradox. It is not just that human beings have in practice so colonised the earth that it is hard to find anywhere untouched by our presence, but that we have done things to the earth, which in the long run will have repercussions for every living creature. Yet there remains a deep-seated longing to encounter, and relate to, nature in the raw, nature as other than ourselves, nature as a source of awe and wonder. My first task therefore must be to set out more fully what this concept of the otherness of the world of nature means, and has meant, in practice.

THE OTHERNESS OF NATURE

A lament about the loss of otherness was the main theme of a book, published in 1990, with the dramatic title *The End of Nature*.[2] The author, an American journalist, was moved by his realisation that the increase in atmospheric carbon dioxide is different in kind from other forms of environmental pollution, in being universal, irreversible, and unpredictable in both its short-term and long-term consequences. By itself this may not seem too alarming. More than ten years since the book was written, the debate continues about whether atmospheric change matters or not, and if it does, how far the majority of people and their governments are prepared to do anything about it, particularly in that author's own country.

Dire warnings about the end of nature are not a new phenomenon. In the Victorian age there were fears that the growth of the railways would bring it about.[3] Railways certainly changed the world, and helped to pollute it but, rather than spelling the end of nature, they gave more people than ever before the opportunity to experience its glories at first hand. If our prodigal way of life were to face us eventually with grievous environmental and social consequences, optimists are happy to predict that new skills will be found, and new technologies developed, to combat new ills. The world has suffered countless catastrophes and mass extinctions, but living things seem to have an almost infinite capacity to adapt to changed circumstances. From this larger perspective the end of nature is not in sight. Even the ultimate horror of a nuclear holocaust would not be the end. There would always be some form of life which could exploit the new environment, however desolated. Nature is much more resilient than the prophets of doom generally allow. But when all this has been said, the author, in using his deliberately provocative language about the end of nature, had something rather more subtle in mind, something more closely linked to our human perceptions of nature and our feelings about it.

He was in part reminding those of us who live in the West that we are the heirs of, and participants in, an extravagant culture which for several centuries has lived wildly beyond its means, and that we form a privileged section of humanity which has indulged in a monstrous exploitation of the world's natural resources. These are familiar and well-justified moral charges. But beyond the dangers and disadvantages which may attend the consequences of atmospheric change, there is a further moral dimension. One of the implications of such change is that no part of what we now call nature can any longer be separated from what human beings have done to it. Even the rain and the sunshine are no longer just there, sheer facts independent of us, but we are forced to wonder whether they are aspects of a new pattern we have inadvertently created. This, claims the author, entails a tragic spiritual loss. It diminishes the sense that our lives are set within something greater than, and distinct from, ourselves. The natural world is losing its quality of otherness from us. 'By changing the weather, we make every spot on earth man-made and artificial. We have deprived nature of its independence, and that is fatal to its meaning. Nature's independence *is* its meaning; without it there is nothing but us.'4 We even have to create wildernesses.

An American might expect to feel this more strongly than a European. The poet Rupert Brooke, for instance, visiting the Canadian Rockies shortly before the First World War, felt uneasy about the country's lack of human history. 'There walk, as yet, no ghosts of lovers in Canadian lanes. This is the essence of the grey freshness and brisk melancholy of this land. And . . . it is the secret of a European's discontent. For it is possible, at a pinch, to do without gods. But one misses the dead.'5 To live in a very old culture is to be reminded again and again that virtually

[55]

My candidate to the professor
Ted Rick explored it to
write the History of the Hudson's Bay
Company.

nothing around us has remained unaffected by the presence of human beings. The immigrant American experience, by contrast, was of an encounter with a natural environment in almost pristine condition, and many have a deep longing to recapture that experience. This is presumably what inspires millions to drive off in their camper vans to remote places, some of them, no doubt, secretly nursing the hope that at the end of the trail they will also find a McDonald's. The author is right, though. We have lost something, something spiritually important, a universal loss which extends to the very composition of the air we breathe.

I have dwelt on this book because it expresses movingly one radical concept of nature, as that which is simply there, apart from us, in some respects alien to us, and like the raging sea able to demonstrate to us our littleness and impotence. Much of the pleasure afforded by the endless succession of wildlife films on television derives from this sense of a largely unknown and fascinating world out there, in which other creatures live their own lives, heedless of the fact that we are watching them. I suspect that part of the attraction of blood sports lies in the competitive encounter with creatures which are truly wild, and which therefore have to be studied and respected if their ways are to be properly understood. (Drag hunting in comparison with fox hunting is a mere paper chase.) And the same seems to be true of fishing and rough shooting, both of which arouse comparable emotions. But the otherness of nature can also evoke the opposite reactions – fear and disgust. Seamus Heaney, in his poem 'Death of a Naturalist',[6] described how as a boy he loved playing by a pond and collecting frogspawn, until one day,

> ... The air was thick with a bass chorus.
> Right down the dam gross-bellied frogs were cocked
> On sods; their loose necks pulsed like sails. Some hopped
> The slap and plop were obscene threats. Some sat
> Poised like mud grenades, their blunt heads farting.
> I sickened, turned, and ran. The great slime kings
> Were gathered there for vengeance and I knew
> That if I dipped my hand the spawn would clutch it.

The young naturalist quickly renounced his vocation, as what had once been friendly and familiar suddenly revealed another face.

The Romantic poets seem to have had the same kind of experience in reverse, particularly in their encounter with those parts of the natural world which had not yet been tamed and organised. Early in the eighteenth century mountains had been widely regarded as ugly, repellent, and superfluous, 'monstrous excrescences on the face of Nature'. By the end of the century they were evoking awe, terror and exaltation, no longer heaps of stone, but pathways to God. And not only mountains. Wordsworth claimed that even as a child he had glimpsed a kind of holiness in the world of nature. Coming back from school at the age of six, the Wanderer

> In solitude returning, saw the hills
> Grow larger in the darkness; all alone
> Beheld the stars come out above his head.
> . . . In such communion, not from terror free,
> . . . Had he perceived the presence and the power
> Of greatness.[8]

It was still possible in those days to experience some parts of nature, even in Europe, as if they continued to bear the marks of their creation, like newborn children 'trailing clouds of glory'.

The 'as if' is important because, from another point of view, it seems obvious that the concept of nature in its pristine state itself bears the marks of being a human construct. In describing something as pristine we implicitly compare it with something else. How, for instance, can we lament changes in the composition of the earth's atmosphere unless we know what the atmosphere is, and what its composition has been, and what it ought to be if our familiar weather patterns are to be sustained? The proof of global warming depends on the sophisticated analysis of highly variable temperature fluctuations, but though people have always been conscious of heat and cold, the concept of temperature itself was only invented in the seventeenth century. Mountains may be pristine in the sense that nobody has yet climbed them or even admired them, but in reality they are constantly changing. Thus at every stage we are dependent on interpretation, and scientific discovery, and preconceptions about what is normal, all of which are culturally conditioned. The construction of an idea of nature is essential before we can know whether and when we have made some kind of difference to it. Nor is it just the natural sciences which impose their interpretations, and change our understanding of what it is we are encountering in what we call nature. We have only to consider how it has been regarded in different cultures to see how strongly conditioned our supposedly instinctive, 'natural' feelings really are.

There is an obvious illustration in the Old Testament. Different attitudes towards nature seem to have been among the factors in the long drawn-out struggle between the worshippers of Yahweh and the various forms of fertility religion already established in the land they were to occupy. The picture is complex and controversial, not least because of conflicting evidence about the historical events underlying the stories of the Exodus, and differing opinions about the extent to which Israelites were already in Canaan before their religious distinctiveness began to become apparent. But these historical complexities need not concern us because, however things came about, both the distinctiveness of Israel and its assimilation into the local culture were for many centuries undoubted facts of life.

A useful indicator of this distinctiveness is the contrast between different attitudes towards sexual activity as an integral part of religious practice. In the Canaanite cults there is clear evidence that sex was mythicised, with human copulation as part of the religious ritual necessary to ensure the fertility of the soil. Thus human sexuality was called into the service of different processes within the natural world, in so far as these were believed to be controlled and cared for by the god, or Baal, of a particular locality. The God of Israel, on the other hand, stood beyond the polarity of sex,[9] just as he stood beyond particular localities and all that went on in them. He was believed to be the creator and owner of the whole land, the prosperity of which depended, not on a fusing of the human and the earthly, but on obedience to a transcendent law. The prophet Hosea, for instance, made much use of sexual imagery. Israel is condemned for saying 'I will go after my lovers, who suppply me with food and drink, with my wool and flax, my oil and perfumes . . .' to which Yahweh replies, 'She does not know that it was I who gave her the grain, the new wine, and fresh oil, I who lavished on her the silver and gold which they used for the Baal . . . They sacrifice on mountaintops and burn offerings on the hills . . . That is why your daughters turn to prostitution and your sons' brides commit adultery.'[10] Faithfulness to the transcendent God of Israel should have meant that the divinisation of sex in the interests of earthly fertility was not only forbidden, but theologically inconceivable. Yahweh was simply not the immanent kind of God, deeply implicated as Baal was in natural processes. He had created them and set them in order, yes, but his presence and power were attested by historical events, not by a kind of sexual sympathetic magic. 'When Israel was a youth, I loved him; out of Egypt I called my son; but the more I called the farther they went from me . . .'[11] The God of Israel and the gods of the people of the land represented two different cultures and two different concepts of the natural world.

That, at least, was the theory. In practice, though, the whole situation was much more muddled than this simple contrast implies. Rather than wholesale rejection of Canaanite religion, its rituals and festivals were incorporated in countless ways into Israelite religion, after appropriate reinterpretation in the light of Israel's history. The brute realities of the natural world are too close to human life to be disregarded in religious practice altogether. Thus in the amalgamation of traditions we can see the outlines of a concept of God as both transcending nature, and as immanent within it, a dichotomy which has analogies with our own ambiguous status as both observers and participants. Sexual practices, of course, were only part of the picture, but they provide a sharply defined focal point around which to draw the contrast. It is no surprise that still today they loom large in any discussion of God and human nature – a point to which I shall be returning in the next chapter. Meanwhile we need to note a further implication from the conflict between these two religious cultures which, confused though they were, tended to polarise theologically between transcendence and immanence.

An excessively one-sided emphasis on God's transcendence of nature can be correlated with a similar view of human beings as standing apart from, and over against, the natural world. This can in turn lead to a strong sense of nature's otherness, not the romantic or mystical otherness already described, but something much colder and more distant. It has often been held responsible for the belief that the right attitude towards nature is to conquer it. The natural world, on such a view, can be seen as doubly separated from God. It is both created and fallen, the damaged arena for the divine drama, not part of the drama itself. Expelled from Eden, human beings have had to struggle against thorns and thistles, and to till a now unsubmissive soil. Nature therefore has to be beaten into shape to serve human purposes. Couple this attitude with the belief that, despite the fall, human beings are innately superior to all other creatures, and the justification for exploiting nature seems all too obvious.

Most Christians today would want to deny this interpretation, and there is indeed plenty in biblical tradition to contradict it. But it also contains a kernel of truth. There is an ambivalence already present in the biblical creation story where everything is pronounced good, yet human beings are given potentially damaging powers over it, the 'dominion' referred to in Genesis 1:28. The significance of this concept has been vigorously debated, and there is a compelling case for saying that human dominion over the earth should entail responsible stewardship, rather than conquest. The transcendent God is heard most clearly, we are told, in the still, small voice, rather than in the wind, fire and earthquake.[12] It is love not power which ultimately conquers. On a true understanding of creation, God transcends nature by giving it to his creatures, and allowing it to be itself. Nevertheless it has to be admitted that a one-sided emphasis on God's transcendence, often making use of the concept of dominion, has at times helped

Even Dawkins is a little like it's!

to promote, or been invoked to justify, destructively exploitative attitudes. And there have been other morally serious people, besides transcendentalists, who have felt it necessary to go to war with nature, among them prominent Darwinians like T. H. Huxley, who were morally repelled by the very process of evolution which they knew had brought them into being.[13]

Whatever the motive, conquest and exploitation are facts of Christian history. Furthermore all civilisations have in their different ways changed the face of the earth, consistently maltreated animals, eaten their bodies, used their strength, and exterminated many of them. Without such exploitation, life as we now know it would not have been possible. The same desire to exploit was one of the original motives for science. Francis Bacon, the father of the experimental method, saw its aim as 'to endow the condition and life of man with new powers or works'. He brilliantly summed up the paradoxical key to such power in his aphorism that 'we must command nature by obeying her laws'.[14] Knowledge, in short, is power, and knowledge grows by treating nature as a set of objects for investigation, a Cartesian machine, rigidly separated from the observer who stands outside it. I have earlier pointed out some of the shortcomings of this concept of natural science, and the fact that we are not as detached from our study of nature as we think we are. The vision of nature as ripe for conquest, however, can override such cautions, and the actual powers made available by scientific discovery have massively reinforced the assumption that it can be moulded at will. A science-based culture, in fact, no less than some forms of religious culture, can shape our perceptions of, and attitudes towards nature. There is no such thing as a pure encounter with its otherness.

Poor old Descartes — he always gets it!

THE SOCIAL CONSTRUCTION OF NATURE

The conclusion that we read into the world of nature many of the feelings and perceptions with which our culture and our history have equipped us, may seem massively obvious. It is worth considering a few examples, however, if only to illustrate how pervasive this process of social construction really is. Just as religion and science have had their share in it, so have ordinary developments in language. Think, for example, what underlies the simple act of looking at a landscape. Leaving aside the worries expressed earlier about the effect of atmospheric changes, it might seem that in admiring a Scottish glen, or a Yorkshire moor, we are viewing nature in the raw, responding to what was there long before any human beings were present to see it or colonise it. But even if it is more or less virgin country, to see it as landscape is a surprisingly modern experience. The word derives from Dutch painters in the sixteenth century. They and their artistic successors have taught us through their pictures to recognise what we now call 'the picturesque'. To be part of an aesthetic tradition in which landscape painting has played a major part, is to be sensitised to those aspects of nature which would make, as we say, a good picture. Hence the impulse to photograph them. The concept of landscape, in other words, acts as an interpretation of nature in the light of a particular cultural history. 'Scenery' has similar origins – this time from the theatre. Both are terms which imply a relatively detached viewpoint, that of spectators outside the action. People who in real life made their living off the land, however aesthetically atractive it might be, were generally not so affected by the look of it. They were more concerned with the quality of the soil, and the health of the trees, and the inconvenience of rocks and cliffs and barren hilltops. Others, more conscious perhaps of history, may see the emptiness of the Scottish landscape in more political terms, as tragic evidence of ancient wrongs.

One of Henry Fielding's novels shows us Parson Adams travelling in the same carriage as wealthy Mr Pounce. Adams observes that it is a fine day.

> 'Ay, and a very fine country too,' answered Pounce. – 'I should think so more,' returned Adams, 'if I had not lately travelled over the Downs, which I take to exceed this and all other prospects in the universe.' – 'A fig for prospects!' answered Pounce; 'one acre here is worth ten there; and for

my own part, I have no delight in the prospect of any land but my own.'[15]

In short, the same scene may be perceived through very different eyes. It may also have been created with different degrees of artifice. English forests were once regarded as a waste of space, savage and dangerous places, to be cleared as rapidly as possible. In the seventeenth and eighteenth centuries planting restarted for economic reasons, because trees were needed for fuel and ships and houses. But landowners were also busy replanting for aesthetic reasons, creating great avenues to mark the importance of the house on which the avenues converged. Alternatively trees could be planted in clumps to enhance the view, or to block out someone else's. A well-planted estate spoke, too, of prosperity and permanence, because trees are planted mostly for the next generation. The love of landscape, particularly as seen from great houses, also gave an impetus to the building of balconies. A balcony is the architectural epitome of observation from a privileged position without being involved.

Simon Schama's fascinating book *Landscape and Memory*[16] has much to say on the history of such changes in the perception of nature. He catalogues in great detail different national and historical responses to woodland, water, and mountains. Forest landscapes, for instance, have particular resonances in Germany, where folk religion and mythology have drawn heavily on the ancient history of the German tribes as forest dwellers. Forests have been a strong feature in German art, they have been symbols of national identity, and it is ironic that the most successful exploiters of these feelings, and hence the most diligent conservationists, have been the Nazis. The savagery and mystery of natural forests seemed to accord with a regime which wielded power by drawing on the darkest and most primitive emotions.

Gardens, too, can speak eloquently of the culture in which they were created. The so-called 'English Garden', which became popular in the eighteenth century even on the Continent, was in many ways a conscious expression of Romanticism. Its deliberately cultivated wildness and irregularity signalled a rejection of the excessively formal gardens of the previous century, and with them a rejection of that century's excessively mechanised God. Some of today's television gardening experts are equally eloquent of a culture in which 'making a statement' and 'being myself' are the primary considerations.

There is another way of looking at landscapes. In 1794 William Smith, a young surveyor for a canal company, climbed with some companions to the top of the tower of York Minster and looked towards the hills where I now live, some twenty miles away. From their shapes and the directions of their slopes he was able to predict what strata would be found beneath their soil. To an eye trained in the study of canal cuttings, a landscape was more than just a view; it was an encitement to discovery. The incident was perhaps the first scientific demonstration in the yet unborn science of geology.[17]

The fact that the concept of landscape has so many ramifications, historical, aesthetic, political, scientific, economic, and personal, should act as a warning against over-simplifying other manifestations of nature in their distinction from ourselves. Landscape is perhaps a rather obvious example of social construction, but one has only to think of human reactions to different animal species to realise that it is not unique. There are good social, biological and historical reasons why most people fear crocodiles more than they fear cows. Nevertheless in terms of intrinsic worth how is one to judge between what are the most ancient and successful of major predators, and what is a humanly bred species of great practical usefulness? Whether it is simply in the way we view them, or whether it is by what we have done to them, our perception of animals is to a greater or lesser degree a social construct. And likewise with the remainder of the natural world.

What we have done to the world of nature has been sometimes to change it, but always and everywhere on earth to leave on it somewhere our own fingerprint. Perhaps nowadays it is only at sea, or in the remotest places on earth, and when we can forget about universal atmospheric pollution, that the full otherness of nature can be experienced, and even there our mobile phone and the communication satellites overhead are reminders that civilisation is not far away. Humanly released radioactivity has already reached Antarctica.

It is by no means a new thought that the very language we use to describe the world of nature is itself a form of social construction. There is a nice premonition of it in the biblical story of Adam naming the animals.[18] In being named they become distinct entities, just as a child learning language begins to separate out its jumble of sensory experiences into things. Edwin Muir draws out the significance of this process in his poem 'The Animals'.[19]

> They do not live in the world,
> Are not in time and space.
> From birth to death hurled
> No word do they have, not one
> To plant a foot upon,
> Were never in any place.
>
> For with names the world was called
> Out of the empty air,
> With names was built and walled,
> Line and circle and square,
> Dust and emerald;
> Snatched from deceiving death
> By the articulate breath.
>
> But these have never trod
> Twice the familiar track,
> Never never turned back
> Into the memoried day.
> All is new and near
> In the great unchanging Here
> Of the fifth great day of God,

That shall remain the same,
Never shall pass away.

On the sixth day we came.

And that made all the difference. The world experienced as an
ordered whole is the product of language. To imagine, therefore,
that it can be known apart from the human construction we
learn to put upon it, is to pursue an abstraction. Our mental
perceptions, shaped by the use of language, and immersion in
the prevailing culture, set the parameters for what we see, and
how we react to it.

One possible basis for the growing sense of responsibility
towards nature may lie in this increasing consciousness of mutual
dependence. We human beings are utterly dependent on the
ordinary processes of nature for our survival. Our lives have
the roots of their being in what is other than ourselves, and there
is nowhere else to go. Yet it is also our world, a world we can
at least partially understand, a world indelibly shaped by us, and
increasingly dependent for its ability to sustain us on human
manipulation. We have also become uneasily aware of the
damage we can do, not only to it but to ourselves. Hence
the strong self-interest in trying to find some agreement on what
kind of restraints and initiatives this mutual dependence should
actually entail.

ENVIRONMENTALISM

The modern use of the word 'environment' cuts across the dicho-
tomies I have been describing, and with them the distinction
between nature and culture. What environs us is both the physical
reality in which our lives are set, and also the accumulated history
of manipulation and interpretation, which are no less powerful
in shaping our lives. I have been arguing that the two are inseparable. What is new in the past fifty years is the growing recognition
that this composite environment, both physically and culturally,
is changing in ways which are potentially harmful. Physical

concerns have tended to predominate. But it has become increasingly clear that the root problems are also cultural, in that different cultures make different environmental demands. Moreover these problems are compounded by the fact that there is no one thing which can be described as 'the environment'. There are generalisations which can be made about such global matters as the use of resources and atmospheric changes, but there is another sense in which each organism lives in, and to a limited extent may create, its own environment;[20] and what is good for one may not be good for another. Mosquitoes and human beings, for instance, have quite different ideas about the desirability of stagnant water. Calls to protect the environment, therefore, raise the inevitable question, Whose environment? It applies not just to different human interests, but to the whole living world. Not that these are entirely distinct, given the extent to which the complex network of living things is so tightly interrelated in all its parts.

The concept of 'sustainable development' has the merit of by-passing some of these complexities, by its implication that all environments need in some measure to be safeguarded. It gained international currency with the publication of the report of the World Commission on Environment and Development in 1987, and has remained the most widely used statement of environmental goals. It aims to get the balance right between what we do to nature, and what in the long term we allow it to be. It is also politically realistic in acknowledging everyone's desire to better themselves, while at the same time tempering these desires by the constant reminder of longer and wider perspectives. Thus industrial and economic development, for instance, are generally to be welcomed, provided they do not limit the opportunities for future generations, or other peoples, to make similar progress. In practice attention has tended to focus on pollution, the use of non-renewable resources, and the threats to biodiversity. The inclusion of the latter is a reminder that sustainable development is not just about long-term human satisfaction, but should be undertaken in a way that allows all forms of life the space in which to flourish. Hence the need to sustain a wide range of native habitats, or at least suitable environments, in preference

THE CONCEPT OF NATURE

to preserving endangered species in zoos. Whether organisms like the smallpox virus should qualify for this kind of protection, is one of those theoretical questions to which broad statements of goals are generally unable to give a consistent answer.

In short, sustainable development could be described as a reasonably realistic model for attempting to live off the world's natural income rather than off its natural capital. The model's inherent weakness is that like it or not, non-renewable capital resources such as fossil fuels will eventually be used up, and therefore not everything we do now is sustainable. Nevertheless, against that can be set the claim that in the past it has always been possible to replace one worked-out resource or technology with a new one. Whether it is credible to suppose that this will continue to be so, depends in part on hopes about what will be technically possible in decades and centuries to come, and in part on the time frame within which people actually care about such matters. On the whole perspectives tend to be relatively short. As John Passmore pointed out in one of the early explorations of this theme, people's future horizons do not usually stretch far beyond their own grandchildren or great-grandchildren.[21] While there is moral force, therefore, in the ideal of sustainability, it is not obvious that it is potent enough to counteract the impetus behind continuously accelerating growth, against which Passmore also issued this warning as long ago as 1974: 'If the liberal democracies collapse, this will be because they have aroused in their citizens aspirations which no society will ever completely satisfy . . .'[22]

In the late 1990s I had the privilege of membership of one of the Government's think tanks, the Round Table on Sustainable Development – now defunct. It became clear from this experience that the concept does indeed have some political clout. It is not too ambitious. It can provide the basis for achievable goals. And all the arguments in favour of sustainability can give due place to the central role of self-interest, both in development and in conservation. The Round Table's task was to give practical advice, both to government departments, and to other tiers of government and industry. For its members it served as a thorough

initiation into the enormously complex problem of making necessarily radical ideas politically acceptable, and turning them into
workable proposals and concrete results. Not surprisingly the
main blockages at government level occurred in the Treasury.
Despite this, sustainable development has won a few modest
successes, and on the global level the international agreement on
carbon emissions is an example of this kind of thinking. But as
we now know such advances are easily undermined in face of a
determined lobby, as shown by the repeated failures in British
transport policy, the popular outcry against rising fuel prices,
and American intransigence on the subject of carbon dioxide
emissions. Part of the difficulty is that self-interest, especially
when it is the self-interest of privileged minorities, is notoriously
shortsighted, whereas conservation programmes can achieve little
except in the long term. Again, self-interest tends to be narrow,
whereas one of the most urgent environmental issues is to give
proper attention to the needs of the vast majority of the world's
population, who have as yet had few benefits from world development. Unless it is undergirded by something more morally or
politically compelling, and a more positive vision of the kind of
world we want it to be, the concept of sustainable development,
though valuable, is unlikely to be able to withstand serious opposition when real vested interests are at stake.

A more radical approach would be to go beyond the attempt
to limit damage, for governments to acknowledge a responsibility
for the natural world as a whole, and thus to take steps towards
managing the planet as a whole. A famous conservationist hand-
book published in 1985 had the grandiose title *The Gaia Atlas
of Planet Management for today's caretakers of tomorrow's
world*.[23] At the time it seemed an inspiring concept, and in the
intervening years management as the answer to all problems has
moved even more into the forefront of modern consciousness.
The sub-title 'Caretakers of tomorrow's world' is not far from
the now much-trumpeted stakeholder economy. It is also reminiscent of the age-old religious theme of stewardship, which is
still central to much Christian thinking about these matters.[24] A
personal sense of responsible stewardship can certainly motivate

And what do individuals actually do.

changes in individual behaviour, and if this were to be translated into responsible corporate behaviour, the results might be dramatic. But *management*? How does one manage a planet, or extend caretaking beyond the relatively trivial? And *who* manages in a world so divided, and when the policies to be decided are so heavily laden with highly contentious political and cultural baggage? Apart from the crushing sense of political unreality, is it fair also to detect a kind of hubris in the idea that the management of nature is even a possibility, still less a desirable answer to its problems? It is dangerously reminiscent of the old ideal of conquest, itself the source of many of today's environmental catastrophes.

The paradox in all this is that the more we subject the environment to our management skills, the more we are likely to destroy the very qualities which make it interesting – its residual otherness from us, its ability to be itself, its naturalness. We might turn the world into a game park and bring back quaggas from the dead, we might clean up our seas and rivers and rid ourselves of pests, we might cut out pollution and waste, and run Earth plc as a super-efficient business, we might even one day be able to control the weather, but do we really want a Disney world, spruced up for human consumption? The real challenge is much harder than that – namely to undertake a radical change of direction, not so much for our sake, but for the sake of nature itself, especially as we become more conscious that the nature we want to conserve has already lost much of its otherness in becoming more and more subject to our own powers of manipulation and interpretation. In religious terms, nature has become desacralised, and a managed world would only be a further step in the same direction.

A very different, and even more radical, approach to the paradoxes of our human relationship with the natural world would be to move in the opposite direction by taking acceptance of the autonomy and otherness of nature to its extreme limit. It has been expressed in the concept of biocentricity.[25] A biocentric world is one centred on life as a whole, not on our particular relationship with it. It is one in which the community of life as

[70]

a whole is treated with respect, because each individual member is seen as having inherent worth. To think of the whole of life as a community is not itself radical or unfamiliar. All living things, including ourselves, are related to one another as part of the evolutionary process. Also, to a greater or lesser degree, all depend on one another for survival. Human beings are dependent on bacteria, for instance, no less than many wild animals are now dependent on us. This tight-knit web of life is not necessarily a balanced and stable one, in fact it is subject to ruthless competition and startling change, as well as mutual support. But all life has enough in common to be a distinct order of being within the rest of nature. Ruth Page in her book *God and the Web of Creation* has described what she calls 'the companioned world'.[26] The companionship is primarily with God, but no less with all other living things, which in greater or lesser degrees share in that relationship. From a non-religious perspective E. O. Wilson expresses much the same point in his celebration of biodiversity.[27] Life is to be valued precisely because of its endless and fascinating heterogeneity, of which we ourselves form a part.

Thus far biocentricity contains no great ethical or political surprises. The radical step in the argument follows from the claim that what distinguishes living things from non-living things is that each living thing has inherent worth. Worth is different from value. Value implies somebody doing the valuing, whereas worth inheres in the thing itself. In the light of its own nature, it is claimed, every form of life pursues its own good in its own way, and its worth lies precisely in this individual pursuit. We are not far at this point from Aristotle's much derided description of life in terms of purpose. Whatever the scientific propriety of this description, in a discussion of ethics the notion of purpose is surely both proper and relevant, as is Aristotle's insight that each living thing strives to fulfil its purpose. It would thus seem to follow from the claim that each living thing is of worth to itself, that it not only does, but also has a right, to pursue its own goals. What might this mean in practice? If our own subjectivity provides a valid clue to what living things as a whole are like, it may well be that even in the simplest forms of life there is a kind of inwardness which gives the idea of an organism being 'of worth to itself' some meaning. This need not imply consciousness, still less self-consciousness, except in the more intelligent animals, but it does give some content to the word 'struggle' in the phrase 'struggle for existence'. Life in its broadest sense is *about* self-preservation, a notion which implies that there must in some very rudimentary sense be a self to preserve. A plausible case can thus be made for taking seriously the claim that each living thing is of worth to itself. In addition, to acknowledge this worth powerfully restores a sense of the sheer givenness and otherness of the whole web of life in which we are involved.

The final step in this argument is even more radical and controversial. If all life is of worth to itself, whose point of view should be adopted when the worths of different manifestations of life are compared? The most radical answer is – nobody's. Biocentrism in its extreme form requires that within the community of life all should be respected for what they are, and human beings should have no privileged position. Its logical conclusion is that since we have done more damage to the world than any other species, and are now its main predator,[28] the web of life might be better off without us, or at least without so many of us.

This is not a solution to environmental problems which is likely to commend itself, but the challenge of this way of thinking highlights the crucial significance of our evolutionary relationship with one another, and forces us to ask what it is that makes us think we are superior to all other forms of life. Thoroughgoing evolutionists these days no longer talk about the evolutionary tree, with ourselves as the topmost branch, but prefer the analogy of the evolutionary bush on which all branches are equal but different. A bush does not have a leading shoot, so why should nature? Nor is it enough to point to our distinctive human qualities. Other animals have their own distinctive qualities. Birds fly better than we do, a dog's sense of smell is incomparably superior to ours, cheetahs run faster, insects are more numerous, bacteria survive better in hostile environments. Our powers of reasoning give us a versatility other animals lack, but within the community of life why should this quality, in contrast to all other qualities, give us a title to superiority, particularly when it has also given us the dangerous freedom to multiply excessively, and to destroy environments outside the normal constraints of competition between species?

It is a question which can only be answered, I believe, within a more comprehensive vision of why there is a world at all, and what our place in it might be. These are theological matters, to which I shall be returning in the final chapter. My immediate purpose has been to illustrate a range of attitudes towards the natural world, and their implications for the way we treat it.

As we have already seen, those who regard themselves merely as detached observers, standing as it were outside nature or above it, are likely to think of it in purely instrumental terms, as a set of objects to be used, manipulated, and changed at will. I have pointed out the connection between knowledge and power in the origins of science, and the consequences this has had for the kind of world we now inhabit. But there were implications too for the way scientists themselves behaved. My own subject, physiology, had a barbarous history in its early years, with dreadful experiments performed on living animals before the days of anaesthetics, and apparently without much thought given to what they might be suffering. It is easy to understand the moral outrage which eventually gave birth to more humane procedures – still not humane enough in the eyes of many. But the scientists were not unique. What they were then doing was only one example among many of an essentially callous attitude towards non-human nature, which in the Western world was rooted in a sense of detachment from it.

The extension of an instrumental attitude towards nature to include human nature itself, can have equally dire results. To treat people as objects ripe for manipulation is to dehumanise them, the first step towards destroying them. The power of reasoned objectivity may be our greatest gift as human beings, but to exalt it over every other human quality is a disaster, as the Romantics were never tired of pointing out. Remove a sense of intimate relationship with the world of nature, remove feeling and instinct, remove an awareness of one's own bodiliness and sexuality, and one is left with half a person – and a dangerous half at that. To believe that one has conquered one's own nature creates a strong temptation to try to do the same for everyone else. One kind of domination leads to another, and we are back to the idea of a rationally managed world, which so attracted the thinkers of the Enlightenment.[29] To express such misgivings is not to denigrate reasoned objectivity. In many respects the world could do with more of it. But there are consequences to detaching it from its wider context in nature as a whole.

To go to the opposite extreme, and see ourselves as participants in nature on an equal footing with every other form of life, would also have unwelcome consequences. Human life as we now know it can only be sustained by the massive exploitation of other life forms. A simpler and less destructive way of life could only be feasible if there were to be an enormous decrease in the human population. Unless it happened as a result of some major disaster, this, like the policy of rational detachment, would require a degree of central control and management on a planetary scale which would be deeply destructive of other human values.

It is also doubtful whether human beings, apart from a few exceptional people, can realistically think of themselves as in no way superior to other life forms. Jainism provides an example of some who do. It professes extreme respect for all life as an article of faith, a moral imperative which is closely linked with belief in the transmigration of souls. If in different reincarnations souls can inhabit different life forms, there is a clear case for not discriminating. So seriously is this policy adopted that a Jain monk, so I have been told, will not travel by air for fear of inadvertently causing the death of insects swept into the jet engines. But the ordinary follower, though vegetarian, has no such inhibitions because the religion itself acknowledges that its highest standards could not be made universally applicable. As the basis of an environmental policy, therefore, even this most radical of all religious forms of biological non-discrimination is limited in its effect. Jainism and in a less extreme form,

Buddhism, are interestingly explicit examples, though, of the extent to which a religion can govern its followers' perceptions of, and attitudes towards, the natural world.

The sensible middle ground, which I suppose most people occupy, tries to hold together, both the givenness of the natural world in its otherness from us, and also our responsibility towards it as those who are part of it, and who increasingly possess the power to make it what it is. Innumerable practical policies try to hold the balance between these two poles. For any of them to work without submission to planetary management, the crucial necessity is to identify adequate and appealing motives for self-restraint. I have already indicated the large role played by self-interest, and I accept that for viable political policies to succeed an element of self-interest is inescapable. But there is also vision, the need for a way of thinking about nature and about ourselves, which pays equal attention both to respect for what is given, and to a sense of responsibility for what might be. The holding together of such themes is a familiar task in most religions, which is why religiously inspired respect for nature need not be limited to those who believe in reincarnation, but should have profound resonances with what is believed about Nature's God, the subject of my final chapter. Meanwhile to conclude this chapter I shall anticipate the specifically religious interpretation of nature as God's creation, by considering a few Christian attempts to inspire workable environmental policies.

NATURE AS CREATION

In his 1984 Gifford Lectures on *God in Creation* Jürgen Moltmann promised 'An ecological doctrine of creation.' His starting point was that God limits his own transcendent powers and enters into fellowship with his creation. He described nature as creation in the making, as needing liberation, and as having a huge unfulfilled potentiality. In the phrase 'creation of heaven and earth', earth represents the here and now, while heaven symbolises the openness of creation to God as the source of endless new energies and possibilities. With God at the centre, neither anthropocentrism nor biocentrism can adequately describe our place in the world.

> The human being is not the meaning and purpose of evolution. The cosmogenesis is not bound to the destiny of human beings. The very reverse is true: the destiny of human beings is bound to the cosmogenesis. Theologically speaking, the meaning and purpose of human beings is to be found in God himself, like the meaning and purpose of all things. In this sense, every single person, and indeed every single living thing in nature, has a meaning, whether they are of utility for evolution or not. The meaning of the individual is not to be found in the collective of the species, and the meaning of the species is not to be found in the existence of the individual. The meaning of them both is to be found in God.[30]

Such an uncompromisingly God-centred vision, combined with an awareness of a global fellowship created to give glory and delight to God, might certainly help to inspire in believers a lively respect for the whole of creation. It can, however, like much theology, seem very distant from everyday concerns. The more is the pity, then, that Moltmann made no attempt to spell out any of its practical implications. In fact the book is notorious for its only concrete suggestion about environmental action – the proper observance of the Sabbath as a day of ecological rest for nature, 'a day when we leave our cars at home'.[31]

By contrast the World Council of Churches has for many decades been prolific in offering practical advice on environmental issues, but less successful in providing a generally agreed theological rationale for it. I have some personal experience of this, having enjoyed 12 years of direct involvement in various bodies responsible for its environmental policies. In the immediate post-war period when attention was largely focused on reconstruction and the social problems created by rapid technological change, the ideal of a 'Responsible Society' under God proved to be both coherent and fruitful.[32] But as environmental issues began to come onto the agenda in the 1970s, and as the WCC expanded, the picture became more complex. Its social ideal became the 'Just, Participatory and Sustainable Society' – not a slogan to set the pulses racing, but an honest attempt to strike a balance between competing objectives in a world where more and more deprived people were becoming vocal about their needs. Social justice, however defined, is a *sine qua non* in a forum such as the WCC, which depends on the good will of its participants. Popular participation is equally necessary, if hearts and minds are to be changed and policies implemented. The idea of sustainability proved more controversial, mainly because it was the rich countries which stood in greatest need of it, but had enough power to resist it, while the poor countries needed and wanted growth. After six years of struggle the slogan was abandoned, and at the 1983 WCC Assembly there emerged by some mysterious process the formula, 'Justice, Peace and the Integrity of Creation'. It was this formula, particularly the notion of the integrity of creation, now fortunately dropped from it, which the committee I chaired during the 1980s was charged with turning into practical policies.

I cannot say that we succeeded. Not the least of our problems was the fact that 'integrity' has different meanings in different languages, as well as several meanings in English. Thus while it is clear that in some sense the created order is an integrated whole, and needs to be respected as a whole, it is not clear that it has integrity in the sense of being complete, sound, and wholly good. Indeed traditional Christian doctrine has repeatedly stressed the opposite, namely that it needs redemption, alongside its human inhabitants. Moltmann's description of creation as a process, as being inherently incomplete, and of heaven (also part of creation) as symbolising its open-endedness, further underlines the theological difficulties in trying to base coherent policies on the notion of integrity. It could be said in defence of the slogan that it expressed a hope rather than a state of affairs, but even as a hope it tended to perpetuate what Ronald Preston has castigated as 'romance ecology':

A kind of homeostatic situation is being suggested in which everything in nature is so related to everything else, that to 'interfere' with it at any point is to upset the whole and create disorder; it is an expression of the hubris and anthropocentricity of twentieth-century humans.

In another incisive essay Preston disposed of some 'ecological fables', among them the beliefs that 'Nature is benign and harmonious' and that 'Indigenous people are superior conservationists'.[33]

As a source of inspiration, therefore, the idea of the integrity of creation had its limitations. What provides motive enough, I suspect, for most Christian believers is a much more diffuse sense that, because God cares about creation sufficiently to redeem it at huge cost, we should care about it also. In my committee we expressed this concern, not so much by deducing principles of action from abstract concepts, but by applying the lessons learnt through sharing in local endeavours to tackle specific environmental problems. We were able to use the prestige of the World Council to arouse local enthusiasm, and then to use these local success stories to inspire others. A project on deforestation in Costa Rica was typical of the kind of work which could be done in this way, and which left in its wake some much better informed and more enthusiastic environmentalists.[34]

The reasons for being concerned, say, about deforestation in a particular part of the world are likely in large measure to relate to its impact and consequences in that area, though they almost certainly gain force by being seen as part of a global movement. In terms of motivation, therefore, it is probably unrealistic to try to be too fussy. Any or all of the motives I have discussed in this chapter may play their part. Human actions are usually fairly muddled. There was a time, for instance, when the best psychotherapists did not have to decide whether they were Freudians, Jungians or Adlerians, but used whatever techniques and insights seemed best to suit the needs of individual patients. Nature is protean in its complexity and variety, and needs a similar complexity and variety of care. Though it is surely right constantly to remind ourselves of its interconnectedness, there is perhaps no need for environmentalists to take a position on such concepts as stewardship, sustainability, ecological management, bio-centricity, theocentricity, and even integrity, as all in their right contexts may provide useful guides to action. The process of negotiating between different needs, hopes, desires, insights and commitments, continues indefinitely. It is also worth observing that while the strongest motivation is frequently the threat, or memory, of disaster, the constant message of the Christian gospel is that there are alternatives to the blindness, greed, mutual suspicion, and ruthless competitiveness, by which many human disasters are precipitated.

Finally, and perhaps most directly relevant of all, it is possible to observe in many cultures, and to draw on, a deep reservoir of affection for natural things, even for quite unlikely ones.[35] In Laurence Sterne's *Tristram Shandy*, Uncle Toby, though an old soldier

> had scarce a heart to retaliate upon a fly. – Go – says he, one day at dinner, to an overgrown one which had buzz'd about his nose, and tormented him cruelly all dinner-time – and which, after infinite attempts, he had caught at last, as it flew by him; – I'll not hurt thee, says my uncle Toby, rising from his chair and going across the room with the fly in his hand, – I'll not hurt a hair of thy head: – Go, says he, lifting up the sash, and opening his hand as he spoke, to let it escape; – go, poor Devil, get thee gone, why should I hurt thee? – This world surely is wide enough to hold both thee and me.[36]

FOUR

FOLLOWING NATURE

In the previous chapter I described an attempt to restore an extinct species, the quagga, by selective breeding from its near relative, Burchell's zebra. The attempt has been successful in that there are now animals which look more or less as quaggas used to look. But, I asked, are they *real* quaggas? Does the fact that they are not directly descended from quaggas make any difference? And how can we be sure that they behave as real quaggas used to behave? There is no way of knowing with any certainty how much of that behaviour was directly dependent on genetic inheritance, and how much was learnt. We know that quaggas went about in herds, and must presumably have learnt some of their habits from each other. But even if these were to a large extent genetically programmed, we cannot be certain that in selecting the right genes to make them look like quaggas, we would necessarily also be selecting the right genes to make them behave as such. Stunning reproductions of life among the dinosaurs can disguise the true depth of our ignorance about what extinct animals really did. Experts can make intelligent guesses on the basis of anatomy, habitat, and the distribution of fossils, but actual knowledge of real dinosaur behaviour is, and probably always will be, inaccessible.

The word 'real' in this context begs a question. It presupposes a certain fixity in the nature of things. But is there? It is the extent to which we can rely on any such fixity, discern a basis for it, and use it as a guide to life, that is the subject of this chapter.

In Aristotle's biology to know the real nature of a dog, or a tree, or a human being, was to have grasped the organising principle which makes each of them distinct, and dictates what kind of life they pursue. This was the original meaning of the word 'nature', and it underlies the subdivision of the living world into species, each with its own nature, where 'nature' means not just anatomical form but the whole range of capacities and purposes which make a thing what it is. It is ironic that it should be just this primary concept of distinct and identifiable natures which now looks increasingly doubtful, in the light of the biological revolution brought about by *The Origin of Species*. Darwin himself was notoriously confused about how species are actually to be distinguished. When does a variation become a separate species? Is it just a matter of convenient labelling? Or are species distinguishable by tracing their separate evolutionary lineages? Or is the crucial difference the ability or not to inter-breed? If the latter, what are we to make of horses, donkeys, and mules, and numerous other more recent examples of inter-species fluidity?[1] Despite its foundation text, the theory of evolution nowadays implicitly dispenses with the idea of a fixed number of species, each with its own nature, and presents us rather with a continuum of life, within which boundaries are formed only slowly, and sometimes incompletely.

The discovery that physical life is a continuum invites the obvious question, do behaviour patterns form a continuum as well? In particular, how far does human behaviour, despite strong cultural conditioning, rest ultimately on our genetic inheritance?

A BIOLOGICAL BASIS FOR BEHAVIOUR

The new discipline of evolutionary psychology, a successor to sociobiology, explores the hypothesis that human behaviour must have its origins and roots in evolutionary competition, and hence be encoded in our genes. It looks for correspondences between sophisticated human activities, and what are claimed to be their more instinctive precursors in less complex organisms. The widespread human concern about property, for instance, might be traced back to the kind of innate territorial instinct familiar to us in many animals, most notably in birds. Our so-called aggressive instincts, and the facial expressions which accompany them, have obvious parallels in animal behaviour. Indeed it has been suggested that our high valuation of justice may have arisen out of the need to dissipate anger in response to the facial signals of those who have been unfairly treated.[2]

One of the latest examples of this kind of explanation, in a book called *A Natural History of Rape*,[3] caused something of a furore by its suggestion that rape is not so much a crime of violence, as a natural and widespread sexual strategy for passing on genes, in which the violence is incidental. The thesis originated in a study of scorpion flies, which alerted the researchers to the prevalence of rape in the animal world, and hence to the need for an evolutionary explanation. The depth of confusion possible on this subject was revealed in a review of the book in the *Times Higher Education Supplement*, in which the reviewer wrote:

> The popular perspective on rape, the social science theory, posits that rape is caused primarily or only by 'culture' or social learning, which is presented as a quasi-metaphysical force that determines human behaviour. But, in fact, culture is totally biological – learning from members of one's own species, like all learning, occurs within the living brains of living beings and is guided by learning adaptations.[4]

I find this an astonishingly naive comment. To say that culture is 'totally biological' simply on the grounds that it entails brain activity is like saying that written words are no more than ink on paper. It is to confuse different levels of understanding, to conflate two widely separate layers of the explanatory sandwich,[5] in the interests of an all-embracing reductionism.

To claim that there need to be different levels of explanation, however, does not preclude the search for connections. In particular if evolutionary accounts of human behaviour are to have any plausibility, they must deal credibly with those types of behaviour which most clearly distinguish us from our animal

ancestors. It is one thing to identify an animal-type aggressive-
ness; it is another to understand how a sense of moral obligation
might have developed from what have been rather misleadingly
characterised as 'selfish genes'. At first sight altruism seems the
unlikely product of an essentially competitive evolutionary
process. However an ostensible advance in understanding came
in what is now known as the kin selection theory of altruism,
which demonstrated a possible means by which a biological basis
for unselfish behaviour could have evolved. Given that genes
belong to families and not just to individuals, there may be
indirect genetic advantages when an individual sacrifices its own
life for the sake of those related to it, with the result that some
at least of their common gene pool survives. Altruism, in other
words, can be of evolutionary benefit to one's own kin, and
among social animals may benefit a wider circle as well. On this
level of understanding worker ants and bees live lives of supreme
self-sacrifice.

But can altruism, in this rather restricted sense, really be a
basis for those aspects of human ethical behaviour in which the
good done to others is especially valued when done for its own
sake, rather than for some supposed advantage? A bird warning
other birds about the approach of a predator may be altruistically
risking its own life; but it is not behaving ethically because its
actions are instinctive, and it is highly unlikely to have considered
any alternatives. Nevertheless it is possible to see how in animals
with stronger social bonds a more deliberate, and hence more
ethical, form of altruism might have developed out of what are
essentially non-ethical biological impulses, through the necessities
of social interaction; and how with the growth of self-awareness,
the social demands on behaviour might come to predominate
over the biological. As Michael Ruse has put it:

> Laid on top of our selfishness is our (genuine) altruism, put
> in place to make us efficient biological 'altruists': a very
> necessary adaptation, given that we humans have so firmly
> gone the route of sociality. We are loving and kind and

generous – really loving and kind and generous – because this is just as much a part of our nature as is our selfishness.[6]

In short, while biology may provide some of the groundbase for ethical behaviour, human culture and the choices made within it are the indispensable context for its development. It is only within human cultures that actions can be designated as good or evil, right or wrong.

Thus cultural and genetic accounts of behaviour need not be regarded as mutually exclusive. There may be value in becoming more aware of those vestigial elements in our human make-up, no doubt encoded in our genes, which bear comparison with what we can observe in other species. It is likely that our animal inheritance provides the raw material for many of the feelings and inclinations, such as sexual attraction or sociability, on which our moral choices may depend, and knowledge of this inheritance may make us wiser in handling them. But given the huge diversity of behaviour both among different species and within different human cultures, the attempt to trace genetic connections between human and animal behaviour can easily fall into the trap of arbitrary selection. It is not hard to find correspondences, but that is a long way from proving that these are genetically based. It is still further from proving that, even if such connections exist, they ought to have any direct bearing on how we should behave today.

Pascal wrote three and a half centuries ago that 'Man must not think that he is on the level either with the brutes or with the angels, nor must he be ignorant of both sides of his nature; but he must know both.'[7] He was not, of course, anticipating Darwin's discovery that the brute is in us by direct descent, nor was he the first to realise that human beings can behave like brutes. He was simply recognising a radical ambivalence in human nature, which has long been known, but which we are now better able to understand. We do indeed bear the marks of our physical ancestry, though they are hard to distinguish from the massive layers of cultural inheritance without which we would not be human at all.

NATURE AND CULTURE

To be human is to be part of a culture, and in that sense culture itself, as my quotation from Ruse indicated, is natural to us. The point becomes even more obvious when we consider how the most distinctive aspects of what it is to be human – language, art, reason, and religion – belong to human beings as such, whatever their particular culture. They take very different forms, and they depend for their particular expression on growing up within a tradition which is communicated from one generation to the next, but the characteristic types of human cultural activity are universal. This is not to imply, however, that outside the human world there are not more rudimentary types of culture appropriate to less self-conscious forms of social life. The ability to learn from one another is not an exclusively human capacity, and I have already suggested that even quaggas might have picked up from each other some of their behavioural characteristics. Primates certainly do, and so do many other social animals. The close study of animal groups in the wild has revealed the dividing line between nature and culture as increasingly fuzzy.

The difficulty of disentangling one from the other is especially obvious in the study of human individuals. Identical twins have been the primary resource for research in this area, but some of the findings have been strangely anomalous.[8] There are stories, for instance, of identical twins separated at birth and brought up in totally different environments who, when they meet for the first time in adult life, discover remarkable similarities in quite trivial matters, such as the kind of clothes they wear or the food they prefer, matters which on any ordinary understanding would be regarded as purely cultural. There are other identical twins who from the start are quite distinctive individuals and who, even as babies, have radically different temperaments. There are also examples of genetically identical twins who do not even look the same. Whatever the explanation of such anomalies, it seems clear that there is no simple equation between identical genetic inheritance and actual human persons. Human nature is irreducibly complex. It is the outcome of a process which, however we strike the balance, depends on a combination of genes, general environmental influences, culture, experiences both in the womb and outside it and, in later stages of development, individual choices. This is perhaps why there appears to be no limit to human variety.

All of which leads to the question implicit in the title of this chapter, about what could be meant by 'following nature' when our human nature is so complex in its origins, and so varied in its expression. The phrase also further exemplifies the ambivalences in the concept of nature itself.

'Following nature' could mean paying attention to scientific evidence of the kind mentioned in the previous section, 'A biological basis for behaviour'. The 2001 Reith Lectures on *Ageing*, for instance, were packed with biological information which might be used in shaping social policies, giving medical advice, and possibly for reversing the processes of ageing themselves. 'Nature' in this sense is everything capable of being studied by scientists, as discussed in Chapter 2 above.

The phrase could also mean 'following natural impulses', whatever their basis, whether genetic or cultural. 'Natural' in this sense is much more closely tied to the emotions, to what feels right. Nature religions with a strong immanent bias, the modern heirs of Baalism as described in Chapter 3, have come back into favour in our increasingly machine-dominated age. They can include everything from herbalism to witchcraft and woodland frolics in the nude. Their attraction lies in their closeness to nature, conceived as a living force which in some measure indwells the believer. The lifestyles of some modern pop stars follow the same pattern, albeit in a very different context. So did D. H. Lawrence who sacralised sex without civilising it.

For the Stoic philosophers 'following nature' meant exactly the opposite. The stars above and the moral law within were the true face of nature as perceived by reason. Calm detachment from the brutalities and misfortunes of a world which was falling apart, was to be achieved through the contemplation of what was eternal and transcendent. In effect, therefore, to follow nature was to obey the dictates of reason, the highest manifestation of human nature, and to eschew emotion.[9] Centuries later, nature-loving Romantics like Wordsworth likewise found inspiration in the more sublime aspects of the natural world, but inspiration strongly suffused by emotion too. Bertrand Russell in his early years dealt with intolerable emotions of isolation and unreality by immersion in the philosophy of mathematics.[10]

A fourth, and within Christian tradition the most dominant, meaning of the phrase 'following nature' was derived from Aristotle, and managed in some measure to combine all these emphases – a close study of the natural world, human aspirations towards natural fulfilment, and the central importance of reason. It achieved its fullest articulation in mediaeval theology, provided the basis for much of the moral teaching of the Roman Catholic Church, and in more modern forms is still an important ethical resource under the title 'natural law'. It should not to be confused with natural law as understood in the natural sciences.

NATURAL LAW

Natural law is based on the ancient and widespread belief that there are moral obligations, inherent in our humanity itself, which need to be obeyed if we are to be true to our essential nature. In the Western tradition there is an early example in Antigone who, in jeopardising her own life for the sake of burying her dead brother, believed she was obeying a more fundamental law than the law of the land which forbade her action.[11] Aristotle's principle that everything has its purpose, which it strives to fulfil in order to realise its true nature, lent itself to a systematisation of such fundamental laws. Human beings have many seemingly contradictory purposes, he said, some of which we share with all life, even with vegetables, such as the impulse to live and grow; others we share with animals, such as the ability to enjoy sensations. But the distinctive element in human nature is reason. It is practical reason, therefore, based on sound knowledge, and refined by life within the *polis* (the political community), which must judge between other natural desires and impulses in the pursuit of goodness.

These are the bare bones of a theory which in the Mediaeval Church and for centuries afterwards undergirded what claimed to be a universal ethic. Its claim on universal acceptance, however, was somewhat compromised by the fact that it had been extensively Christianised. It drew, for instance, on the concept of divine order as the true basis of sound knowledge. It also provided a Christian equivalent to Aristotle's *polis* in the Church, as the context in which human life could alone find its fulfilment. To obey natural law was to discern the order of one's being, as ordained by God, and to espouse its moral significance in the light of reason, which also owed its being to God. Natural law also found its title deeds in Scripture, most notably in St Paul's comments on those who did not know the law of Moses.

> When Gentiles who do not know the law carry out its precepts by the light of nature, then, although they have no law, they are their own law; they show that what the law requires is inscribed on their hearts, and to this their conscience gives supporting witness, since their own thoughts argue the case, sometimes against them, sometimes even for them.[12]

How far God was necessarily involved in this enlightenment of Gentile consciences has been hotly disputed, and is a key issue in the relationship between nature and grace, a topic to which I shall be returning in Chapter 6. For the moment it is enough to note that rational thinking about morality, however much it might have been buttressed within its Christian context, was nevertheless deemed to be possible within the natural law tradition without explicit reference to revelation. Hence the significance of Aquinas's appeal to Aristotle, in spelling out the order of natural inclinations:

> First, there is an inclination in man towards the good corresponding to what he has in common with all individual beings, the desire to continue in existence in accordance with their nature. In accordance with this inclination those matters which conserve man's life, or are contrary to it, are

governed by natural law. Secondly . . . those matters are said to be of natural law 'which nature has taught all animals', such as the union of male and female, the bringing up of children, and the like. Thirdly, there is in man an inclination to good according to the nature of reason which is peculiar to him. He has a natural inclination to know the truth about God and to live in society.[13]

Aristotle, preceded by Plato, was also the source for the four cardinal (or non-theological) virtues which, like the moral principles derived from human nature, depended heavily on reason. Thus prudence discerns the limits of what is reasonably practical. Justice is about the rational direction of the will towards right conduct. Temperance restrains passions contrary to reason, while courage holds them fast to what reason requires.[14] All this is set by the Christian natural law tradition within the context of a rational, but fallen, world which needs the grace of God (manifested in the three theological virtues, faith, hope, and love) if it is to reach its ultimate fulfilment. Nevertheless, it was claimed, despite human frailty and fallenness, reason remains a reliable guide, and the natural law based on it can thus have universal significance.

Others have not been so sure. Any such attempt to derive ethics from a rational study of human nature poses obvious problems for those Christians who believe that human nature and reason have been so corrupted by sin, that nothing about God's purposes for human life can be discerned except through revelation. As with the relationship between nature and grace, this is a further point to which I shall be returning in Chapter 6, where I shall be suggesting that it represents an over-pessimistic assessment of our rational powers. The strong identification of the natural law tradition with Christianity, though, remains a barrier to universalising it. In modern Roman Catholicism there is a prime example of this problem in its teaching on contraception. Theoretically this is prohibited on the basis of arguments from natural law, whereas in practice these are so inconclusive that the prohibition has to be asserted as binding by appeal to ecclesiastical authority.

But these are not the only problems. What I have said earlier about the way human nature is formed, and the strong influence of culture, indicates difficulties of another kind. How is it possible to distinguish between what is essential to human nature, and what are the mere contingencies of evolutionary and historical development? If the propensity to rape, for instance, really were encoded in our genes, should this be regarded as a God-given capacity requiring fulfilment? Add to this mixed bag of genetic propensities the sheer variety of human types and customs, a variety which becomes more evident as the scope for self-expression increases, and the idea of a universal natural law appears even more doubtful.

There is also the objection, constantly reiterated by Isaiah Berlin, who questioned whether reason is capable of adjudicating between certain aims and values which, as he saw it, are fundamentally irreconcilable.[15] It is worth noting, however, that similar objections have been met in earlier times. Despite his eighteenth-century conditioning, Bishop Butler, one of the greatest of English moralists, knew as much as any man about the complexities of human nature and the inconstancies of human emotions, yet remained firmly committed to belief in an over-riding internal authority, reason or conscience, which could adjudicate between them.[16] It has been said of him:

> Nothing is too small or too trivial to be ignored, nothing too slight to merit the attention of a proper estimation. Butler's faith in God is revealed by the intense reverence for human nature that pervades his ethical writings, by his preoccupation with the problem, which he never finally resolves, of a proper and valid conception of experience as at once revealing to us the unsuspected richness and complexity of our existence, and yet compelling us to acknowledge frontiers which we must not pass . . . We must reckon with human nature as a whole; and yet there is a sense in which the fundamental laws of our being

are immediately and certainly known to the honest and unsophisticated.[17]

Diversity and complexity, in other words, are not necessarily counter-arguments to the idea of natural law, at least in so far as its fundamental principles are concerned. It is these, rather than their applications in widely different contexts, which comprise the heart of the matter as human beings reflect rationally on what they are, and what their lives should be.

The philosophical objection that a natural law theory of ethics appears to derive an 'ought' from an 'is', can be quickly dismissed. The theory is not proposing that the possession of certain natural inclinations common to most human beings entails a moral obligation to satisfy them. Its claim is that rational reflection on what we are and what our inclinations tell us about ourselves, reveals our human nature as inherently placing obligations upon us. The fact that we have strong feelings about social cohesion and fairness, for instance, obliges us to think rationally about justice. It does not mean that what we feel is fair must necessarily be so. Hume, who in effect was the first to draw the 'is/ought' distinction, acknowledged that morality must have its roots in human nature. He saw many obligations as arising quite naturally:

> Mankind is an inventive species; and where an invention is obvious and absolutely necessary, it may properly be said to be as natural as anything that proceeds immediately from original principles, without the intervention of thought or reflection. Though the rules of justice be *artificial*, they are not *arbitrary*. Nor is the expression improper to call them *Laws of Nature*, if by natural we understand what is common to any species, or even if we confine it to mean what is inseparable from the species.[18]

Despite the range of possible objections, therefore, the idea that there is such a thing as human nature, and that it has moral significance, remains impressively persistent. If morality is not to be arbitrary, a mere matter of cultural conditioning, nor to be based solely on disputable religious premises, and if law is to have a rational foundation and an authority beyond the particular dictates of lawmakers, there is a need to identify some truths about what makes for human flourishing, rooted in something more durable than human convention and historical accident.

As we have seen in Hume, the belief that this must be so resurfaced, outside Christian commitment, as one of the key elements of the Enlightenment. In some of its manifestations it had dire results. Isaiah Berlin memorably described progressive French thinkers as believing:

> . . . that a logically connected structure of laws and generalisations susceptible of demonstration and verification could be constructed and replace the chaotic amalgam of ignorance, mental laziness, guesswork, superstition, prejudice, dogma, fantasy, and, above all, the 'interested error' maintained by the rulers of mankind and largely responsible for the blunders, vices and misfortunes of humanity.[19]

Unfortunately the French thinkers left out of their calculations the subtleties of earlier traditions, as well as the seductions of relativism on the one hand, and sin on the other. They also forgot that what reason can propose, reason can refute. Their certainties proved to be as fragile as the systems they sought to destroy.

Edmund Burke, the scourge of this kind of arrogant rationalism, himself appealed to human nature, but he meant by it something much more like the status quo. Nature is what has come to be. It is what has grown, rooted in history. 'The nature of man is intricate;' he wrote, 'the objects of society are of the greatest possible complexity; and therefore no simple disposition or direction of power can be suitable either to man's nature, or to the quality of his affairs.'[20] In Burke's eyes, to appeal to 'nature' as the French revolutionaries conceived of it, was to set the 'feeble contrivances of reason' against the wisdom of the ages. He was appealing to what I was describing earlier as the cultural and historical dimension of human nature. Outside a particular cultural context we are nothing. Aristotle had the *polis*. Aquinas could rely on centuries of Christian culture. Even rationalism had its cultural presuppositions. But when these were gone, what was left was one of the more damaging long-term consequences of Enlightenment rationalism, against which Burke's critique was of no avail – the rise of individualism. Individuals without any stable or meaningful commitment to a particular social order, and (as in many modern cultures) faced with apparently limitless choice, have to ask themselves what reasons they have for choosing one way of life rather than another. Where, if anywhere, are boundaries to be drawn? And what social order can there be without some agreement on the kind of constraints that are necessary and desirable?[21] In a profound sense human culture rests on the ability and willingness to say no.

NATURAL LAW UPDATED

It is time to look afresh at the possibility that there might be a wisdom of the ages, an inextricable mixture of genetic inheritance and historical conditioning, which finds reasonably consistent expression in all human cultures. If there is such a wisdom, it would be foolish to neglect it, given that it must have become an essential part of what human beings are. There are some simple forms of behaviour in which the genetic basis is obvious. Babies learn to crawl instinctively, not as a result of observing their parents. They incessantly explore the world around them because that is what they are programmed to do, not because anybody has told them to do it. The relationship between mothers and babies is the same the world over, and not all that different when the mothers and babies are chimpanzees. A somewhat more complex example is the empathy possible between people of all cultures, a fellow-feeling which can usually manifest itself spontaneously, unless feelings have been deliberately suppressed through some process of dehumanisation or cultural isolation. There seems to be an innate ability to recognise each other's subjectivity, despite huge barriers of linguistic incomprehension. In the light of such examples, and notwithstanding all that I have been saying about the pervasiveness of cultural influences, there really do seem to be feelings, desires, predispositions, and patterns of behaviour which are simply human, given as part of our human nature, and therefore relevant in decisions about what we should do or be.

But there are dangers in trying to be too precise about the contents of this common human inheritance, particularly those aspects of it thought to be located in our genes. The familiar complaint that modern people still have the genetic predispositions of hunter-gatherers, while trying to live in a world totally alien to this way of life, has a grain of truth in it, but not when it is used as a catch-all explanation for the discontents of civilisation, nor when it is applied simplistically to entirely modern phenomena, such as predatory take-over bids. Indeed from what is known about the few remaining hunter-gatherers in our own day, it would appear that even they are not as dependent on predatory genetic predispositions as some evolutionary enthusiasts have suggested city financiers might be. The dividing line between nature and culture is just as difficult to draw in them as it is in us. Much of their lifestyle seems to result from a strong tendency to think of the world as imbued with human qualities. But this is not unique to them. Modern children who personify their dolls and toys do the same, as one of the normal stages in the development of thinking. Nor is hunting and gathering simply about food. It is just as much about constructing social relationships, as is any modern dinner party in which food and sociability are inseparable. An anthropologist living among the Beaver Indians in British Columbia has described a society which is mostly inarticulate, dependent on stories and dreams, but extraordinarily skilful and far-sighted in its ways of maintaining and pursuing its traditional way of life. It was despised, as such cultures frequently are, by an officialdom which wanted to use its hunting grounds for other purposes, but when the two sides talked with one another it was clear that this was a clash of cultures and interests, not between two levels of intelligence or two types of being.[22] The main differences lay in the conceptual tools which the two sides had at their disposal. The

Beaver Indians had a strong moral code appropriate to their circumstances, but which tragically tended to collapse when their time-honoured way of life was destroyed.

Mary Midgley in her splendid book *Beast and Man* has given a convincing defence of the idea of what she calls 'the roots of human nature'. In moving from consideration of our animal inheritance to suggesting the basis for a kind of natural law, she claims that it is possible to discern a 'structure of deep, lasting preferences', which may well differ as between species, and be adapted to the needs of each particular kind of existence.[23] These preferences may be hard to reconcile with one another as, for example, in the conflict between parental care and self-preservation. If your baby is carried off by a lion, for instance, do you chase the lion at the risk of your own life? or do you write off the loss? Our characteristically human way of dealing with such conflicts, especially when they are internal to us, is to weigh them up in our minds, and it is out of this process of thinking and choosing that the integrated personality emerges. Other species may have preferences very similar to our own. Elephants and wolves, like us, really care about their young, and may have to face similar dilemmas concerning them. But to a greater extent than ourselves, says Midgley, they have what she calls 'a structure of motives that shapes their lives around a certain preferred kind of solution'. Their intelligence is of a less reflective kind, and hence lacks the moral significance of the choices which fall on us.[24] Our peculiar privilege and burden is to know, after being faced with such a choice, that we might have done something else.

Moral choice, then, can be both rational and appropriate to our nature, but it depends on identifying the human 'structure of deep and lasting preferences', and the needs which underlie them. The word 'structure' is significant because Midgley is referring to something which belongs to us simply as human beings, without differentiating between our genetic and cultural inheritances. The point is that it is common to us, and displays a kind of givenness. If the preferences were simply a matter of individual choice, then any behaviour might be justified simply on the grounds that that is the kind of person we want to be. The possibilities for disastrous self-deception would be endless. But if our structure of deep lasting preferences is somehow given, it can carry a degree of authority, if only by demonstrating that the neglect or violation of what is fundamental to our human nature carries its own penalties.

How then can we discern this human structure of preferences? Animal analogies may mislead, because we can only know which analogies are relevant, if we do in fact distinguish between propensities which are primarily genetic, and those which are primarily cultural. And this is precisely the difficulty. A more hopeful approach might be to by-pass this problem, and look below the surface of different cultures, to tease out what is implied or required by the very fact of living together, and to see whether there are common values or preferences being expressed. The fact that it has been possible to reach very wide agreement on basic human rights is a hopeful sign that there are indeed commonalities to be found. This approach to natural law has the further advantage that it starts, not from supposedly natural endowments, but from actual shared human preferences, usually expressed in recognisably similar social habits and conventions, the most fundamental of which have now been institutionally enshrined in international agreements. It also avoids the naturalistic fallacy of mysteriously deriving an 'ought' from an 'is'. The 'ought' is already there.

C. S. Lewis mounted a vigorous defence of natural law so conceived in his frequently quoted lectures on *The Abolition of Man*.[25] He argued that belief in a given set of values was an educational necessity, and listed a wide variety of quotations from different cultures and religions to demonstrate that there is indeed what he called 'a universal Tao', a common morality embracing many different traditions. The method has its drawbacks, however, as he himself recognised, in that it appears to be something of a hotchpotch, dependent on the comprehensiveness of the cultural trawl on which it is based.

John Finnis in his book *Natural Law and Natural Rights*[26] has pursued a similar aim, but by a rather more promising method.

He claims to have identified seven basic values which are self-evident, essential, and which are actually found, albeit expressed in many different ways, in all known human societies. It is the self-evidence of the values, rather than their ubiquity, which gives them their authority. The fact that they are found everywhere confirms this authority, but does not, as in C. S. Lewis, provide the basis for it. By a self-evident value Finnis means one which is valued for its own sake as an essential aspect of human well being, without needing to be derived from anything more fundamental. The seven he identifies are life, knowledge, play, aesthetic experience, sociability, practical reasonableness, and religion. Note that these are values, not ethical obligations. Obligations arise from them through a process of rational reflection. Justice, for instance, can be seen as the demand made by practical reasonableness in response to the value of sociability.

Why are these seven values to be regarded as self-evident? The value of life hardly needs justification. It clearly corresponds to one of Midgley's 'deep, lasting preferences', and there is an important sense in which the drive for self-preservation, though not absolute, is fundamental to the existence of all other values. Its practical expression also includes a huge raft of subsidiary values and conventions on matters ranging from health, and the procreation and nurturing of children, to food production and self-defence. To list the actual ways in which the value of life has guided human conduct would be to write a history of human evolution and civilisation. Even those human societies which have seemed careless of life, as for example in the practice of human sacrifice, have implicitly asserted its value as the supreme offering required to safeguard the lives of others.

The value of knowledge is equally self-evident, rooted in the characteristic human desire to question and to explore. As already mentioned, human babies, like most other young animals, have a natural impulse to explore their environment. But to a unique extent they also learn by being part of a culture in which knowledge and skills are passed from one generation to another. Knowledge, in other words, is just as fundamental to all other human values as life itself. It is true that not everybody wants knowledge as such, and there is some knowledge most people might prefer not to have, such as the knowledge of how to make nuclear weapons. There are also those who for a variety of reasons might wish to suppress some forms of knowledge, like the much-quoted Christian group who are said to have prayed, 'O God don't let this evolution be true. But if it is, don't let it be generally known.' Despite such aberrations, to deny that knowledge is a self-evident value would be self-refuting. The sceptic can only do so by claiming to possess superior knowledge about what is to be preferred instead of it.

Of the other values on Finnis's list, play is perhaps the most surprising. Like others, it clearly has biological roots, and in some animals, particularly predators, may be an important element in the honing of their skills. There is recent evidence that in children too it may have an essential role at a vital stage in brain development.[27] But human beings, including adults and even some animals, also play for its own sake. We misunderstand it as a value, and are in danger of distorting its character, if we try to defend it simply on the grounds of its biological usefulness. Its self-evident value seems to lie precisely in the fact that it is not useful. Play, particularly in older children and adults, is a highly significant first step in escaping from necessity. Rowan Williams links it with an illuminating discussion of fraternity, around the idea 'that there are goods to be worked for that are completely different in kind from material goods, goods that exist only in the game, within the agreed structures of unproductive action'.[28] Play, in other words, can enable fraternity by creating opportunities for stepping outside customary social roles, under rules which can be accepted because they are arbitrary, and thus in a larger sense do not really matter. Within this complex of ideas lie the roots of freedom. But this subtle relationship can easily be destroyed, which is why the designation of play as a self-evident value can at first sight seem idiosyncratic. Montaigne said of chess:

> I hate and avoid it, because it is not enough of a game. It is too serious for an amusement, and I am ashamed to give it

an attention that might be employed on some good action . . . See how our minds magnify and exaggerate this absurd pastime . . .[29]

What would he have said, I wonder, about contemporary spectator sports, in which precisely those qualities which give play its value, are apt to be submerged in overblown rivalries and the irresistible pressures of commercialism?[30] At the highest levels of international sport these days the contests are not so much between competitors as between competing technologies. It is a question of who can afford the most advanced equipment, or deploy the best team of, physiologists, nutritionists, psychologists and so forth, or buy the best players. Fortunately we are not dependent on such public exhibitions in order to value play. More modest forms of it have greater moral significance, even such simple examples as a conversational game over the garden fence, in which the human worth of those engaged in it can be affirmed without the constraints of over-seriousness.

As with play, there is a significant place in all human societies for art in one form or another, most commonly perhaps in music. Aesthetically valuable artefacts have been produced for at least 20,000 years. Whatever their precise significance, prehistoric cave paintings and numerous carvings of humans and animals, are evidence of considerable artistic skills at around the time when human society in a recognisable form was beginning to take shape.[31] One of the more recent cave paintings in East Africa even depicts figures playing musical intruments.[32] Clearly what we now recognise as art was important in the ancient world, and it has undoubtedly made a major contribution to human self-understanding in every known civilisation. Is this enough to prove its self-evident value? I suspect aesthetic value is as difficult to pin down precisely as the meaning of the word 'game',[33] but it seems to share with play the value of stepping outside necessity, expressing a freedom to transcend the sheerly given, and providing a perspective from which life can be seen differently. Like play it can be justified as an end in itself. 'High culture,' as someone has put it recently, 'provides a time and place that is not simply here and now.' Prehistoric cave painters may have been trying to manipulate nature, but they did so by a free act of creation. Maybe aesthetic value ultimately resides in just such an expression of imaginative freedom, and in our human response to it. And there may even be an echo of such a possibility in the phrase 'God created human beings in his own image'.[34] It is perhaps significant that this statement is made when all that the author of Genesis has so far told us about God is that on him the whole of created existence depends.

The self-evident value of sociability and friendship is clear from our essential nature as social animals. Our identity as persons is grounded in our relationship with others. What is not so clear, however, is where the boundaries of sociability are to be drawn. How does one pass from family or tribal loyalties to a more general conception of the common good? In biblical times the lessons were learnt only slowly and incompletely, despite the implications of universality in the Hebrew doctrine of God as Lord of all. Even in our own time, with a universal declaration of human rights, increasing globalisation, and far more cross-cultural communication than has ever been possible before, the idea that the good of individuals is inseparably linked with that of the international community, is hard to sell. But perhaps there is a glimmer of hope in what I described earlier as the universal instinctive recognition of each other's subjectivity, no matter what national, social or cultural barriers intervene. Sociability, though fundamental to human nature and culture, may, like goodness itself, have to begin 'in Minute Particulars'.[35]

The importance of practical reasonableness as the central pillar of the classical natural law tradition has already been sufficiently discussed. Here it is only necessary to distinguish it from abstract reason. Its value lies, not in the possession of great intellectual power as such, but in the need to make sensible choices coherent enough to create a sustainable culture, to balance one's commitments, and to devise practical means of putting them into effect. In short, it is the conductor of the orchestra of values. Freudian inspired denigration of reason, and sociologically inspired relativisation of it, cannot undermine its self-evident value, because both depend on practical reasoning to make their case.

Finnis's seventh value, religion, may seem more controversial than the rest. It is included because human beings have always in one way or another tried to relate themselves to invisible powers outside themselves, and to see their lives within an ever larger cosmic framework. In particular the concept of value itself, and the need to reconcile different values, invites the thought that there must be a hierarchy of values, in the discernment of which religious beliefs are peculiarly relevant. Understood in this very general sense, religion can take its place alongside art and play, as enshrining values which point beyond what is merely mundane, self-interested, or self-limited. This is a deliberately modest and generalised description, framed in such a way as not to pre-empt questions about the truth and wide variety of actual religious belief and practice. The point is simply that in any general discussion of values, religious value can claim to be as self-evidently necessary as all the others, and like the other basic values, does not seem reducible to anything else. And despite pockets of resistance it is, in one form or another, as universal as they are. A recent study which makes powerful claims to explain all religion in terms of evolutionary psychology and cognitive science, incidentally bears witness to this universality.[36]

I have drawn on Finnis's structure of values because it seems to me that if there is going to be a theory of natural law at all, it needs to look something like this. It has to be very general. It has to allow for a great diversity of expression. It has to encapsulate what different societies throughout history have in fact found to be enduringly valuable. And it has to have roots in the actual needs, and deep and lasting preferences, common to real people. We can contrast it with attempts to derive ethical principles from abstract concepts of human rationality or, even more dubiously, to base ethical principles directly on the details of human biology or anatomy. Nowhere, unfortunately, has the latter tendency been more prominent than in the discussion of sex.

SEXUALITY – A CASE STUDY

I venture here into the disputed realm of sex and sexuality not because, as we are frequently told, the churches are obsessed by it, nor because, as we are also frequently and rather contradictorily told, the churches are afraid of it, but because it is so fundamental to what human beings are, and nowadays gives rise to some of the most contentious moral issues. It can therefore serve as a useful test case for any viable theory of natural law, and in particular for the practical application of Finnis's seven values.

It has been suggested with some plausibility that the need for social control in general, and for its internalisation as moral self-restraint, began with the need to control sexual behaviour. Indeed so central is sexuality to most higher forms of animal life that standard behaviour patterns, whether instinctive or learned, associated with sexual intercourse, combined with different concerns and modes of conduct as between the sexes, are found not only in primates but to some extent in all social animals. Midgley's 'structures of deep and lasting preferences' may take a bewildering number of forms, but the evidence for some pre-human structuring of the sexual drive and of sexual roles seems clear enough.

In so-called 'primitive societies' the pattern is equally bewildering, but a striking feature in many, if not most, of them is the high importance given to sexual rituals, especially the initiation of boys at puberty into their adult male sexual role. It is as if sexual maturity does not just happen, but has to be conferred, even imposed, ceremoniously by the tribe.[37] Thus the first experience of sexual powers, instead of being individual and furtive, as so often in our present culture, is inherently social and heavily dependent on custom. The tribe is, as it were, insuring itself against slipping back into a state of pre-human nature, where whatever social constraints there may be on sexual activity are latent under an appearance of unrestrained competition. I am no anthropologist, but the description of a distinctively human way of life as emerging *pari passu* with the socialisation of sexuality, seems to me convincing, and it is hard to think of any but the most transient human societies in which sexual activity is not regulated in some form or other. It is no coincidence that the first moral story in the Bible, the story of the Fall, has strong sexual overtones, as does the account of what is purported to be one of the earliest rites – that of circumcision.

The significance of control was the central feature of Foucault's groundbreaking work on the history of sexuality.[38] His thesis was that 'disciplinary power' has so shaped all expressions of sexuality into socially approved forms that it is no longer possible to identify what is 'natural'. In particular he made much of the idea that the escape in the latter half of the twentieth century from so-called repressive attitudes towards sex, has simply replaced one form of disciplinary power with another. The medicalisation of sex, for instance, has been just as powerful in prescribing norms as was the confessional in the seventeenth and eighteenth centuries, and Victorian values in the nineteenth.

The belief that all heirs of Western civilisation are ineluctably trapped under different forms of domination is a seductive one, especially to those who feel themselves in some way oppressed. If this is really the case, though, it is not clear what liberation could possibly mean. In fact if, as Foucault seems to be claiming, there is nothing simply 'given' in the realm of sexuality, any supposed liberation must turn out to be subjection to just another arbitrary form of dominance. To understand how our desires and expectations have been shaped for us by others may be enlightening, but the most urgent question is one which Foucault, from his Nietzschean perspective, cannot answer or even seriously ask, namely whether beyond such external influences it is possible to identify any abiding truths about our sexual nature, and hence about its fulfilment.[39]

It is with this question in mind, therefore, that it may be useful to look again at Finnis's list of self-evident values, and their bearing on sexual control. Remember that it is a list of values, not of rules. The most it can help us do is to set some goals, to describe a framework for sexual fulfilment, on the basis of which practical reasoning can attempt to match policies to circumstances. But even this modest aim is not immune to Foucault's criticism that values may only appear self-evident because they are so deeply entrenched in dominant social assumptions. Or was it he himself who was trapped in his own bottomless relativism, with no vantage point for building any permanent insights or values on what might be claimed as the real ground of our human nature?

Sexual activity has obvious relevance to the value of life, in that without it life could not continue. Not everybody values children, but communities which value their own continuance must do so, and must make arrangements for protecting and nurturing the future generation. This in itself may initiate some sort of social control, but the need for such arrangements does not necessarily imply a positive desire to dominate; it is just a fact of life, because children cannot look after themselves. Nor can they educate themselves, which is why a respect for the value of knowledge is another essential aspect of the generative process.

Knowledge also has more direct sexual connotations, as for instance in the interesting use of the biblical word 'know' to mean 'sexual intercourse'. Though the phrase 'carnal knowledge' is now archaic, it can still be a useful pointer to the intrinsic moral relationship between sex and intimacy, as can the word 'intercourse' itself. Intercourse implies a personal relationship; it is a form of communication, an exchange of more than body fluids. To enjoy sexual intercourse without 'knowing' the other is not only a contradiction in terms, but is to slip back into a pre-human mode. Intimacy also means allowing oneself to be known, and hence to become vulnerable, and is thus an essential element in one of the unexpected gifts of sexual love – the exposure and release of the self. In fact there is a whole cluster of values around the concept of sexual knowledge which, sadly, is all too often treated as if it referred only to a set of techniques.

Just as failure to value knowledge of the other person can tend to dehumanise sexual relationships, so can loss of the dimension of play. Sex is not a wholly solemn business, in fact there is much which borders on the ludicrous. But play, as I have stressed earlier, is not merely about having fun. It is about the transcendence of the mere practicalities of life, which then makes possible the building of relationships not dependent on mutual profit or productiveness. In this light it is difficult to see how a natural law ethic which places a high value on play, could be used to prohibit contraception. On the contrary a recognition of its value could provide grounds for disapproval of sexual relationships intended only to serve practical biological needs, or further dehumanised by being turned into a kind of transaction.

The aesthetic values capable of being expressed within the realm of sexuality speak for themselves. Sex has been one of the main inspirations for art. The curious use of the word 'sexy' to describe anything attractive, interesting, exciting, or beautiful, says a good deal about our contemporary culture. But perhaps we need a reminder that sexual relations themselves should have aesthetic value. There is beautiful, life-enhancing, relationship-creating sex, and there is ugly sex which disgusts, destroys, and abuses.

The value of sociability as the moral context for sexual relationships is equally obvious. It includes, of course, the values of friendship, companionship, loyalty, and self-sacrifice. But it is significant that the social bonding of partners, as one of the aims of sexual intercourse, and inherent both in the concept of knowing and of play, only achieved its present high valuation with the arrival of easily accessible and reliable contraception. This has entailed a major shift in the perception of what sex is for, and hence of the social controls appropriate to it. It has also, contrariwise, demonstrated how sexual sociability by itself, when unhampered by other values, can quickly revert to pre-human forms. The prophet Jeremiah was sensitive to the point in his description of how 'each neighs after another man's wife, like a well-fed and lusty stallion'.[40]

Practical reasonableness may not be very evident in much that goes on in the name of sexuality, but it is the essential quality needed to relate different values to each other in the interests of personal integrity, and to translate them into action.

As for religious value, the complex relationship between sexuality and religion almost certainly extends back to the earliest attempts to regulate sexual activity. I described in Chapter 3 how Israelite religion had to distinguish itself from the fertility cults which surrounded it, but also took something from them. This is only a tiny fraction of a long and complex story, which it would be out of place to try to tell here. The main point is that there have been different histories of the relationship in different religions, but that all have been concerned about it, and that within the Christian faith this history has sometimes been glorious and sometimes tragic.

My purpose in this rapid review has been to suggest that all seven of the values identified by Finnis can throw a distinctive light on the moral issues surrounding sexuality. Between them they provide a broad moral landscape within which sexual conduct, as well as all other types of behaviour, can take their bearings. To that extent they can be validated in practice. While not claiming that the list is exhaustive, the implication is that there really is such a thing as our sexual nature, to which natural law is relevant, but that its ethical significance is multi-dimensional and cannot be adequately discussed under a single aspect, or in a single cultural context. It is not as if procreation, or pleasure, or social stability, or creative excitement, or personal fidelity were all that is at stake. If the seven values really are self-evident, and thus fundamental to our human nature, an ethic based on natural law needs to take them all into account and to find a reasonable balance between them in the light of particular circumstances. They are a reminder that sexuality is pertinent to the whole of what we are, and to all the values by which we seek to live. Much that seems wrong today in both the public and personal treatment of sexual matters can be traced to a failure to give all seven values their due weight. Though Finnis himself says little about sexuality, I find it encouraging that his analysis is so clearly applicable. Of course, it may be that other values beside those he has identified will, on further analysis, prove equally important and even self-evident. No scheme of this kind should be set in concrete. What matters is his demonstration that appeals to what is inherent in human nature cannot all be dismissed on the grounds that they are arbitrary.

HOMOSEXUALITY

Within the general picture set out above, homosexuality is a special case. It calls for separate treatment, not least because of the frequent condemnation of homosexual activities on the grounds that they are 'unnatural'. In terms of Finnis's analysis, this charge of 'unnaturalness' would seem to be focused on three of his values: life, aesthetic value and, in some of its forms, religion. Life appears to be devalued by the inherent lack of procreational possibility. Aesthetic taste is said to be outraged by a use of the body in ways which are widely regarded as inappropriate or disgusting. Religious disapproval of homosexuality is by and large confined to the Semitic religions, and seems to have had its origin in Jewish rules about purity rather than in the moral law as such.[41] Among modern biblical scholars, interpretation of the relevant biblical passages has proved to be highly controversial, thus making them unpromising material for an appeal to unequivocal religious tradition.

In answer to the first two objections it can be said that the lack of procreational possibility is certainly a misfortune, but is not unique to homosexuals. The strict view that all sexual intercourse must be open to the possibility of procreation is, as we have seen, defended by those who hold it on the basis of natural law; but it is widely acknowledged that the defence is no longer convincing, not least in the light of the other values already discussed.

Aesthetic distaste at what is regarded as biological misuse raises more difficult problems, but is commonly met by the counter-claim that what seems unnatural to one person may seem natural to another. This, however, is a superficial use of the word, which confuses different senses, thereby obscuring the key question of whether it refers to more than personal likes and dislikes.

If the claim that there is a genetic predisposition to homosexual orientation were to be substantiated, this would strengthen the argument for it as one of a variety of given elements in human nature. At present no direct genetic link has yet been proved nor, as I have repeatedly stressed, are genes the only basis for what counts as natural in human beings. The abundant evidence of same-sex relationships in the non-human world has also been cited in favour of naturalness. However this, like all other direct arguments from animal to human behaviour, is double-edged. Its moral significance depends on whether or not human sexual encounters are to be regarded as distinctive in expressing values besides the satisfaction of immediate biological desires, as well as in restraining desires which run counter to these values. The large remaining areas of ignorance about the causes of homosexuality provide further reasons for being cautious in deciding what is or is not 'natural' in this context. It seems best therefore not to pre-empt judgements about naturalness, but to tackle the aesthetic objection on its own terms.

The perceived distastefulness of some homosexual practices is at first sight no more conclusive than arguments about unnaturalness. Tastes undoubtedly differ, and may be hard to reconcile. But does it follow from such differences that there are no criteria by which anything more than highly personal aesthetic judgements can be made? One possible criterion in this context might distinguish between different intentions. To do something disgusting, knowing that it is disgusting and delighting in it for that reason, is generally regarded, not only as an expression of bad taste, but as demonstrating some kind of moral deficiency. There are, of course, artists who see it as their role to shock and disgust in pushing out the boundaries of awareness, and they justify themselves on the grounds of wanting to awaken people to reality. Even if their argument is accepted, I am not sure that indulgence in what is recognised to be disgusting can muster the same defence, when it is simply a matter of individual pleasure. In the latter case some important judgements about what is valuable in life seem to be missing, and there would seem to be something seriously wrong with a natural law ethic which advocated disgustingness for its own sake. This objection fails, however, when disgustingness is not intended, and when morally responsible people see aesthetic value where others do not. It is one thing to defend aesthetic value in general, but quite another to absolutise a particular aesthetic judgement about practices one does not share. Apart from this vexed question of what people intend when doing something which appears disgusting to others, it thus seems to me that aesthetic value, like Finnis's other self-evident values, cannot be used to draw a decisive and convincing moral distinction between homosexual and heterosexual practices.

The nub of the moral and political arguments about homo-sexuality lies elsewhere. It concerns homosexual practice in its aspect as a cultural phenomenon with its own codes of conduct, its own patterns of interpersonal relationships, and its own interests in practical matters such as the education and upbringing of children. In Classical Greece, where pederasty was normal, the explanation for its prevalence is usually sought in social structures, in the separation between the sexes, for example, or the relationship between tutors and their adolescent pupils, within which sexual initiation was an expected part. But nobody suggests that most Greek men were homosexuals, incapable of being anything else. In fact effeminate homo-sexuals were despised. In predominantly Christian cultures, where historically homosexual practice has for the most part been driven underground, its very existence has often been denied. This has been especially true in Africa, and I recall immense difficulties in the 1980s in trying to persuade African church leaders even to discuss homosexuality as the dangers of AIDS began to become apparent. The strength of feeling which still exists on the subject of homosexuality in many parts of Christian Africa found vigorous expression at the 1998 Lambeth Conference, and opened up a serious division within the Anglican Communion on questions of biblical interpretation. But I suspect that cultural and historical motivations were at least as important as the ostensible theological differences.

In a generally tolerant culture it is difficult to know for certain what underlies an individual's sexual orientation, how far it is genetically driven, how far external pressures contribute to it, and whether there is a real element of personal choice. The massive 1994 report on *Sexual Behaviour in Britain* provided striking evidence of the fluidity of sexual orientation, and concluded that although homosexual experience is quite widespread, 'exclusively homosexual behaviour is rare'.[42] Uncertainty about one's sexual orientation may be a normal part of growing up, but there can be cultural inducements, too, when a particular marginalised lifestyle turns militant, and thus becomes a useful means of signalling sexual independence. Alternatively being part of a homosexual culture may be seen as an emotionally safe form of behaviour at an age when the other sex appears dangerously different. The pressures on young people to experiment are very strong, and frequently strengthened still further by the notion that in order to make sensible choices they need to be taught about all possible permutations and combinations of sexual activity. It is small wonder that the public discussion of homosexuality in recent years has frequently been confused and inconclusive, and that public debate should have centred on pieces of legislation which are largely symbolic. The transition to a state of affairs in which sexual orientation is no longer seen as the defining characteristic of a distinct cultural group, but as part of normal variation within a single culture, would ease many of the tensions, and reduce the need for the stridency which at present aggravates them.

Let me stress that I have been considering the matter from the perspective of natural law, which has a greater role in public debate and legislation than does Christian revelation. Many Christians would doubtless want to say more, but I have already hinted at the difficulties in interpreting the comparatively small number of biblical passages which refer to homosexuality. Not only is it hard to know precisely what was originally meant,[43] but there are problems too in judging how far this was conditioned by the special circumstances of a particular culture, very different from our own, and how far much more recent circumstances have further conditioned modern attitudes. The only certainty is that we know a great deal more about homosexuality than any previous generation, though that cuts little or no ice with those who believe that religious and moral truths are revealed once for all. It seems to me that within the churches arguments about homosexuality are set to continue, and that the answer probably lies in greater concentration on those other obligations under natural law, such as intimacy, fraternity, fidelity, knowledge of and sympathy for one another, and spiritual values, which do not figure so widely in the public debates.

Natural law gives clearer guidance in relation to sexual abuse. It is of the essence of abuse that it is destructive of relationships, and that it is degrading rather than life-enhancing. Though it may sometimes masquerade as play, it does not contain the priceless element of free and equal participation characteristic of play at its best. It is also necessarily secretive, and thus internally damaging to both the abused and the abuser. A type of experience which depends on secrecy and has to be hidden away, either through fear, or shame, or disgust, cannot be integrated into life. So it merely festers, and eventually destroys. It is perhaps significant that even in ancient Greece the treatment of boys as sexual partners seems to have been a cause of anxiety, judging by the amount the philosophers talked about it. It must have been hard for thoughtful teachers who had exercised their power over a boy destined to become a free citizen, and used him as an object for their pleasure, to reconcile this domination with a proper respect for his dignity.

Yet even here a kind of natural law seems to have been at work. There is a line to be drawn between freedom and its abuse. There really do seem to be values which belong to human nature as such. And there is a price to be paid for not respecting what we fundamentally are, what our evolution, and our history have made us, and for neglecting to give due weight to our extraordinary human capacity for transcending our biological origins.

It is a pity that the [...] have got so confused about [...] sexuality of obsessed [...]

FIVE

IMPROVING NATURE

Human beings are inveterate improvers. The strong pressure to explore and devise new ways of doing things is one of the marks of human intelligence. Admittedly this has not always been as obvious as it is today. It seems to have taken more than a million years for our pre-human ancestors to improve their method of manufacturing stone handaxes. The next stage of advance, lasting a mere 200,000 years or so, reveals a growing use of intelligence in the more careful selection of stones, and more sophisticated methods of knocking them into shape. It was only with the arrival, some 100,000 years ago, of *homo sapiens*, and still more brainpower, that the real acceleration began, visible nowadays in the increasingly numerous and complex artefacts which eventually became the main evidences of civilised life.[1] From then on it is a story of ever-increasing success in adapting nature to human ends. But though the modern world can boast of staggering powers over nature, these do not in themselves imply greater intelligence. It has been the steady accumulation of knowledge and the refinement of practical skills, rather than increased intelligence, which in recent centuries have given the human race such dominance. A major turning point was reached in the nineteenth century with what A. N. Whitehead called 'the invention of the method of invention', the systematic technological exploitation of science-based discovery. This is the key which has unlocked such huge potential for innovation, and has today created for us a world almost spinning out of control, as new products and possibilities are generated faster than our intelligences can assimilate or assess their full implications.

The widening gulf between our human ability to control the natural world for our own ends, and our ability to use these powers wisely, is a reminder of the inherent ambivalence of the concept of control itself. More control in one area of life frequently entails less control in another, as when individual freedoms have to be restricted as a direct consequence of technological advances. In the previous chapter I floated the idea that one of the earliest signs of specifically human culture, with all the new powers at its disposal, might have been the imposition of social constraints on sexual behaviour. There can be no culture without some kind of ethical control over its members, without established practices which define the group and set it apart from others. It seems equally true that in almost all circumstances the control of nature requires an element of social co-operation.

The taming of fire is an obvious example, whether one is thinking of the controlled burning of vegetation, which has to be a co-operative effort, or the common hearth as one of the earliest evidences of human habitation. There is also the importance attached by Lévi-Strauss to cooking as a marker of the transition from nature to culture, in view of the degree of social organisation necessarily entailed by it.[2] Cooking clearly distinguishes human beings from other animals, as well as being a fertile source of social differentiation. Roasting, for instance, is said to be socially more prestigious than boiling, because it is more wasteful of precious juices. Fire itself, though, does not have to be understood scientifically in order to be culturally significant, any more than the processes of reproduction have to be understood scientifically in order to control sexual activity. But scientific understanding enormously increases the possibilities of adapting both for the better service of human ends. Our modern concerns arise from the fact that, while human beings have always tried to improve on nature by controlling it, the expansion of knowledge has now given us such powers that urgent new questions, and new kinds of question, have to be asked about how, and on what basis, these powers can themselves be controlled.

Agriculture is another example. In its earliest forms it stabilised control over the food supply, thus leading to the establishment of settled communities, and eventually to the growth of cities, and so to all the gifts of civilisation which flow from living together and sharing responsibilities. Improvements in control and production through breeding, through the invention of agricultural implements, and through better care of the soil, also set the scene for large increases in population. But it is worth noting how slow the changes were, and how recently some of the now familiar improvements arrived in parts of the world which might have been expected to be more inventive. The value of planting crops in rows, and weeding thoroughly between them, for instance, was known in China in at least the sixth century B.C. It was not practised in Europe until the eighteenth century.[3] A possible reason for the difference is that improvements in efficiency could be promoted and propagated much more rapidly in a bureaucratic society than in a feudal one. Similarly in many parts of the world today subsistence agriculture continues, not primarily through ignorance, which is remediable, but because patterns of land tenure impede the adoption of more efficient methods. Social patterns of control, in other words, may be as critical to success as technical knowledge. We are now discovering, to many people's alarm, that in the face of really big and rapid technical changes, such as the proposed use of GM crops, social factors, even in supposedly scientifically orientated cultures, may prove to be decisive. They were clearly a factor in the disasters which befell British agriculture at the beginning of this century as a result of BSE and foot-and-mouth disease. Whatever the precise causes, it seems to have been the character of modern agricultural markets which helped to create the circumstances in which such diseases could get out of control, while technical methods of combating them proved relatively ineffective.

FREEDOMS GAINED AND LOST

These indications of ambivalence in the idea of control over the natural world are part of the paradox of freedom itself. It is rare to gain freedoms without at the same time losing some, or to be able to choose without at the same time rejecting. Hence the importance of such questions as, who exercises control? and who benefits from it? Do we know enough about some new potential power to be sure of its possible costs and dangers? At one level, ever-growing technical mastery over nature has given many people unprecedented freedom to order the pattern of their own lives, but has not been matched by a corresponding growth in social awareness and responsibility. In developed countries the majority of people now live in an environment which, in almost every aspect, has been controlled and improved to make for ease of living and to widen our choices. But the price paid for this is a high degree of dependence on social structures and processes which may not be as stable or reliable as they are assumed to be. A fuel blockade can rapidly demonstrate how vulnerable the support systems of industrialised countries really are. Indeed it has become increasingly obvious that, even apart from dreadful errors like BSE, our new freedom to shape the natural world to suit our own ends can have unwelcome consequences. Some of these might be classed as nature fighting back, some entail massive social changes and the imposition of new forms of social control, and some raise profound ethical issues. My concern in this chapter is mainly with this third category, the ethics of 'improvement'. But before developing the theme, let me give some brief examples of the first two.

Before retirement I used to live in a house, the oldest part of which, the basement, was built in the early thirteenth century. Like many old houses it was sited near a navigable river, which now is only ten yards away and thirteen feet down. Next to the basement door is a series of flood marks, with dates. It is clear from these that in the last two centuries successive floods have been getting higher, so much so that my predecessor and I both kept a boat in the basement. On one notable occasion when the level of floodwater was approaching the main fuse box, he rang what was then the Central Electricity Generating Board to ask what he should do. 'On no account, your Grace,' was the reply, 'should you attempt to walk on the water.'

Why have the floods got worse? Global warming might have something to do with it, but almost certainly the main reason is that over the years the river has been 'improved' by a lock a few miles downstream, by increased flood protection in York upstream, and by better drainage in the hills from which most of the water comes. During my twelve years there, we had two major floods, and duly added marks higher up the wall. My successor will by now have added a still higher one.

I cite this as a small, but personal, example of the unintended effects of changes which may in themselves have been desirable. On a vastly larger scale one can think of the disasters which have followed the building of dams in environmentally sensitive areas. Turkey's new dams, giving it control of water supplies over a huge area, are already exacerbating the political problems of the Middle East. Hydroelectric dams almost anywhere can create a conflict of interest between the needs of electricity production and the needs of farmers downstream. It has been claimed that the holding back of normal flow during the dry season can be a major cause of subsequent flooding, as appears to have happened in Mozambique.[4] In other parts of the world some of the floods and mudslides have probably been unleashed by deforestation, and global warming may even have caused hurricanes in Hampshire. In theory we ought to be able to calculate the consequences of our actions. In practice we do not seem to be very good at it, particularly in complex natural environments. Nature still has the capacity to take us by surprise.

For my second category – the unwelcome social consequences of the exploitation of nature – we need look no further than the ever-expanding legislative jungle within which modern life has to be lived. The taming of fire, for instance, has now been extended to the extraction, distribution, and use of natural gas, a marvellous improvement on collecting sticks from the local forest, but one necessarily hedged around at every stage by complex and detailed regulations. Its use also makes demands, not always fulfilled, on the safety consciousness of everyone who has anything to do with it. The same is true of agricultural weed control, as weedkillers and pesticides are substituted for the time-consuming labour of hoeing between straight rows of plants. Regulations over GM crops are likely to be even more stringent and far-reaching. Even that great symbol of twenty-first century freedom, the Internet, is beginning to explore legal safeguards as its potential for fraud and unwelcome intrusion becomes more apparent. In short, there seems to be a repeated pattern whereby every technical advance brings a corresponding increase in legislative control, and a renewed demand for responsible personal use.

One of the sad truths underlying this pattern is that in practice it is frequently unwise to trust people not to abuse or misuse the enormous powers which, in an industrial society, allow us to exploit nature according to our own individual desires. If our environment is largely self-created and if, apart from when faced with disasters such as earthquakes and fatal disease, we have come to think of nature as an instrument, subject to almost unlimited manipulation for human ends, and if there is no acknowledgement of strong moral constraints or of a moral authority outside ourselves, it is not clear where, other than in the efforts of legislators, the constraints on our behaviour will in future lie. The only answer seems to lie in more and more complex forms of legislative coercion. Such legislation, we may hope, will usually be devised by well-meaning people concerned to protect some freedoms at the cost of others. But the legislators are themselves in difficulties as they are required to make definitions in more and more complex areas of life. And in any event, laws are clumsy instruments for dealing with often delicately balanced issues, especially those which are not yet well understood. How, for instance, can one define precisely in law the distinction between proper and improper uses of human embryos?[5] Hence the importance of my third category – the need for widely accepted ethical criteria by which to tackle such questions, as well as informed public discussion about what are genuine improvements, and what are not, and what the social and environmental costs of them are likely to be.

I suggested in the previous chapter that there may still be some bases for constraints on human behaviour in the form of self-evident values, which are seen to be rooted both in our physical nature and in the experience of all actual cultures. These are not as stable as we might wish, however. The physical factors which might otherwise constrain us can seem less significant the greater the emphasis on 'improving' nature, including our own nature, to suit our own ends. The validity of cultural traditions, meanwhile, is progressively undermined by the growing tendency to write off the past as no longer a relevant source of guidance in a rapidly changing world – indeed in many instances as a positive hindrance to human fulfilment. We are thus left feeling the need of a value system robust enough to counteract the disruptive impact of ever greater manipulatory powers, when ironically it is the very exercise of those powers which is changing our concept of what it is to be human. I am not encouraged by the exuberant words of a molecular biologist, one of the initiators of the human genome project:

> The old dreams of the cultural perfection of man were always sharply constrained by his inherited imperfections and limitations ... The horizons of the new eugenics are, in principle, boundless. For the first time in all time, a living creature understands its origin and can undertake to design its future ...[6]

There are echoes of Nietzsche in the bald and bold assertion that humanity can re-create itself, a kind of romanticism which thinks it can transcend history. What sort of future can we expect, I wonder, under a regime in which the old constraints have disappeared, and the idea that there might be self-evident values is discounted? Science at its best ought to teach us humility, especially when it reminds us what latecomers we are within the world of nature. But if the message is that we can remake ourselves in whatever image we choose, and if there is no acknowledgement of any source of moral authority outside ourselves, how can a proper humility be learnt, except through the kind of disasters which expose the actual limitations of our knowledge, our human incapacity to use it wisely unless we are coerced into doing so, and nature's propensity to upset our plans?

The limitations are deep-rooted and, to illustrate both the technical and social problems which designing our future is likely to entail, I take the obvious example of genetic manipulation.

THE NATURE OF GENES

One of the most readable popular accounts of the history of genetics, from its birth as a science to the start of the project to spell out the entire human genetic code, was unfortunately given the wrong title – *The Human Blueprint*.[7] Genes are units of heredity, and were believed to exist on the evidence of experiments in breeding, long before anybody knew what they were. But now that so much more is known about their composition and how they actually work, it is clear that the genetic code is not a blueprint of the animal to which it gives rise. In reality it acts more like a set of instructions. The difference is not pedantic, but crucial to an understanding of what genetic manipulation can realistically be expected to achieve.

In a blueprint there is a one-to-one correspondence between the details as represented in the design and the details of the finished article, such that a particular line or circle directly specifies the manufacture of an edge, or hole, or whatever. In following a set of instructions, however, there is no such direct correspondence. The finished article emerges as the result of a procedure, with one process building on and modifying another, in such a way that a tiny alteration in one instruction may lead to a completely different product, just as a small word like 'no' might change the whole course of a life.

This dependence on instructions rather than blueprints is what makes it possible for quite small variations in genetic structures to generate such an enormous diversity of living forms. The fact that we human beings share some 98.4 per cent of our genes with chimpanzees is constantly quoted as evidence of our close relationship. It looks less impressive when set alongside the 75 per cent or so that we share with nematode worms. No doubt we have the same basic metabolic processes and the same segmental structure in common with worms, but that is about the sum of it. Palaces and hovels may both be built of the same kind of bricks. A process of development based on instructions can give rise to very simple structures or to vastly complex ones, with only a comparatively small number of the instructions directly responsible for distinguishing one outcome from the other. Recent comments, to the effect that we should be humbled by the discovery that the number of human genes may be about half the original estimate, totally miss the point.

The confusion between a set of instructions and a blueprint tends to arise because the first stage of genetic activity does have analogies with a blueprint, in that it is really a form of copying rather than instructing. Genes provide a kind of template for the formation of proteins, and it is the multifarious interactions between these proteins, controlled by the genes, which determine subsequent development, and result in the formation of a human being, say, rather than a chimpanzee. The discovery that very slight differences of coding within particular genes may be responsible for particular diseases, such as cystic fibrosis, or particular attributes, such as eye colour, can further reinforce the misconception that living matter is built up out of a series of bits and processes, as one might build a car from a set of independent parts. But these one-to-one relationships between genes and easily identifiable outcomes are the exception. The reality is more like what goes on in an elaborate social structure, as in a city, where the different units are constantly modifying each other's action. The result is that the same gene may perform many apparently unrelated roles within the total structure which the multiplicity of genes build together. This is why there is need for great caution in replacing or altering genes, because it is extremely difficult to know in advance what the full ramifications of any change might be.

There is an analogy with language. Words need not have invariable meanings, but interact with other words, and may even change from nouns to adjectives or verbs, depending on the context. Take the three sentences:

> James had a fast car.
> James had a fast wife.
> James had a fast.

The sentences only differ from one another by a single word, but the changes require three quite different interpretations of the word 'fast'. Similarly with genes. Their effects depend on what is happening around them. In most instances there is no way of knowing, simply by analysing the genes themselves, what subtle transformations of function might occur under their influence at different stages in the process of development.

The astonishing thing is that this complex series of interactions works, by and large, so reliably. But that is by no means the whole of the story. The development of an organism also depends, to differing extents, on constantly changing interactions with its environment. Making the right connections in the nervous system, for instance, depends partly on external stimulation. The optic nerve will fail to grow properly unless its eye is exposed to light. In general it is not possible to understand the true nature of an organism without also understanding the impact on it of the environmental niche it occupies. Knowledge of internal genetic processes only provides half the picture. In our own case as human beings the crucial importance of what goes on outside us, including the relationships we form, is even more apparent. We not only depend far more than any other animal on learnt behaviour, we are also unique in the extent to which we fashion our own environment. In Chapters 2 and 3 I was concerned to make the point that the world in which we grow up, and to which we respond, is at least in some measure a human creation. In Chapter 6 I shall explore a possible wider meaning of the concept of environment, which has profound implications for what we understand ourselves to be. Here and now my concern is with the way this mutual relationship between ourselves and our environment sets up a kind of feedback system. Like all feedbacks it enormously magnifies and complicates the interplay between the different factors. This is why it is so impossibly difficult to be certain what in our human nature can be ascribed to our genes, and what belongs to the culture and circumstances which have shaped us, and in which we find ourselves. To think of human beings simply in genetic terms is to miss most of the picture.

It is against this complex background of internal and external interactions that any proposals to interfere with human genes, or make genetic 'improvements' to human beings, need to be assessed.

GENETIC MANIPULATION

Leaving on one side the very large fields of genetic diagnosis and identification, it is possible to divide the actual and proposed medical uses of human genes roughly into four main categories:

1. Genetic material can be used *in vitro* for the manufacture of individual proteins which, for one reason or another, the body may not be able to manufacture for itself. For most purposes it is not even necessary to use human genes, because the proteins required are common to most mammals. Much insulin, for example, is made in this way, and the process is relatively straightforward scientifically because it involves none of the subsequent complex interactions between proteins I was describing earlier. It is also ethically straightforward in not being essentially different from any other kind of replacement therapy. The body needs a protein. Genes *in vitro* can provide it. No ethical principles appear to be at stake.

The use of stem cells *in vitro* to grow replacement tissues or, possibly one day, organs, should be similarly uncontroversial.[8] Stem cells are primitive undifferentiated cells from which other more specialised cells, of whatever type is needed, can in principle be grown. Ethical difficulties arise, however, because in the present state of knowledge human stem cells can only be grown successfully from human embryos. A further complication is that, in order to make the new tissues grown from these cells compatible with those of the patient who is to receive them, his or her genes, in the form of a cell nucleus, would have to be transferred to the embryo, and thus to the stem cells to be derived from it. Though this would technically be a form of cloning, its ethical implications are quite different from the cloning of an entire human being; the embryo itself would not be allowed to do more than produce stem cells, which would thereafter be grown in a separate culture; meanwhile the cloned embryo would be destroyed before reaching the legal limit of fourteen days. The proposed procedure has given rise, however, to anxieties about what might be done with the technique once it has been fully developed, which is why the British government has been quick to put a legal ban on cloning as such.

Ethical anxieties about the purely instrumental use of embryos for a technique which, unlike *in vitro* fertilisation, has nothing to do with reproduction, and which entails their subsequent destruction, might be eased by the hope that such use need only be a temporary expedient. It is argued that the research has first to be done on embryonic cells before there can be any realistic prospect of learning how to start from adult ones. If this can be achieved, it would also obviate the need for cloning, since the original cells, from which the new tissues would be grown, could be taken from the patients themselves, and would thus automatically be compatible. Ethical doubts remain, especially since so much depends on hopes about the successful outcome of such research, the results of which are by no means certain. But these doubts are not sufficient, in my view, to forbid the temporary experimental use of embryos as a bridge towards the ultimate goal, with its enormous potential for transforming transplant surgery. British government regulations already allow the necessary research, but without what I regard as the necessary provisos – that the permission should be for a defined period of time, and strictly limited to the development of this particular technique.

2. The name 'gene therapy' is given to a variety of techniques for transferring replacement genes to appropriate parts of the body, in circumstances where defects in an identifiable gene are

known to be the sole cause of some debilitating disease. Cystic fibrosis is the best-known example, and occurs only in children whose mother and father both carry the same relatively common defective gene. The disease is likely to lead to early death, usually from congestion of the lungs. A few thousand other diseases are known to be caused by defects in single genes, but most of them are fortunately very rare. The aim of therapy in such cases is to equip an appropriate micro-organism with the right gene, and send it to the affected site – the lungs in the case of cystic fibrosis – so that it can manufacture the right protein where it is needed. One of the major disadvantages of this form of treatment is that the new gene does not become part of the recipient's genetic structure, and is thus unlikely to reproduce. This means that its effect is only temporary, and the treatment needs to be constantly repeated. The procedure has also revealed some unexpected risks, and has resulted in at least one death. Ethically, though, it is in the same category as the previous examples, as a form of replacement therapy using genes to make proteins which, for one reason or another, the body cannot make for itself. It is not a form of genetic improvement.

3. The same cannot be said of the third category, germline therapy, which would entail the much more drastic step of replacing defective genes in embryos intended to grow into adult human beings. The replacement would have to take place during *in vitro* fertilisation, and it could, if successful, result in permanent cures for all the single gene defects mentioned earlier, both for the patients themselves and for their descendants. But the uncertainties and hazards involved in tinkering with the genetic code during the embryonic stage of development are, in the present state of knowledge, much too great; and the ethical and legal implications of experimenting on embryos destined to develop into human persons, at present rule all such procedures out of court. Some significant steps have been taken, however, in the direction of germline therapy, such as the current genetic testing and selection of embryos during *in vitro* fertilisation. But while this may avoid the hazards of actual genetic manipulation,

it introduces a new range of ethical problems concerning the role of deliberate science-based choice in the begetting of what are deemed to be suitable children – a topic to which I shall be returning under the next heading. The selection of genetically sound embryos in cases where there is a known risk of inheriting a disease caused by a defect in a single gene, seems to me to be reasonable. Sex selection for social reasons, on the other hand, and in the absence of a specific gender-linked disease, seems to me to cross a dangerous frontier.

Meanwhile, still under the heading of germline therapy, it is worth noting that British government regulations now permit, unwisely in my view, the development of a technique known as 'oocyte nucleus transfer'.[9] The aim of this is to circumvent a distressing condition, mitochondrial disease, which is transmitted through small packets of DNA, the mitochondria, which are found, not in the nucleus of each cell as part of its chromosomes, but in the body of each cell, its cytoplasm. These do not form part of the main genetic code, and are transmitted only through the female line because they are not present in sperm, which have no cytoplasm. A suggested means for preventing transmission of the disease would be to remove the healthy nucleus from the ovum of a potential mother, known to have mitochondrial disease, and insert it into the denucleated ovum of a healthy donor. Normal *in vitro* fertilisation could then take place, using this new composite ovum. The baby thus conceived would have chromosomes from both its parents, representing some 95 per cent of its DNA, and the remaining 5 per cent in its mitochondria would come from the cytoplasm of the ovum which had been donated.

The procedure would be extremely hazardous. The transference of nuclei from one cell to another has a very low success rate, which is a major scientific reason why the cloning of human beings should not be contemplated. But because the egg donor's mitochondria would form part of the resulting embryo's DNA, the procedure would also breach the present legal and ethical safeguards, according to which no embryo which has been subject to experimental manipulation is allowed to develop beyond fourteen days. No matter how worthy the motives and desirable the possible end-results, it would in effect be a form of germline therapy, in which DNA is transferred to an embryo destined to develop into a person, thereby undermining the principles on which the present law is based, and paving the way for much more drastic developments.

4. The further step of going beyond the cure of clearly defined diseases, whether caused by single genes or mitochondria, to attempting more general genetic 'improvements', would hugely increase the risk of unintended consequences, and on these grounds alone there are powerful reasons for prohibiting such interference. Genetic interactions are too complex for geneticists to be certain about any but the most carefully targeted and limited interventions. But it is not just safety which is at issue. There are more general ethical objections to what has been called the designer baby scenario, and these apply with even greater force to cloning. Because some geneticists still nurse the ultimate dream that the practical difficulties will be overcome, it is worth considering more closely why these objections to the aim of human 'improvement' are held so strongly.

Nobody knows in advance what difference having a designer baby might make to the relationship between parents and child. Some might claim that, having got exactly what they wanted, they would love the child all the more. What is the difference, it might be said, between bringing up a child the way you want it, and arranging at the time of conception that it has all the qualities you want for it – blue eyes, good looks, a sparkling intellect, athletic prowess, and so forth? My own belief is that manufacturing a child to specification would subtly undermine the quality of givenness which lies at the heart of our respect for one another, and undergirds our sense of each other's independent individuality. It is not for nothing that babies are described as gifts, and as possessing gifts. To have decided beforehand what kind of gift that baby should be, would introduce a proprietorial element into parenthood, when the most pressing need in all children's personal formation is to be accepted, simply and without reserve, for what they are. There is also a vitally important reciprocal relationship between parents and children. Parents, like children themselves, need to grow in maturity and depth as they come to terms with the otherness of those who are dependent on them. It is a learning process all the more necessary in a culture where fulfilling oneself, and being in control of one's own life and destiny, are so highly prized.

But, it might be retorted, some prospective parents deliberately look for a mate who will bear them the kind of child they want and, far from being unnatural, this is what most animals do as well. What is wrong with giving nature a helping hand?

It seems to me that the difference made by genetic manipulation is that it introduces an impersonal, synthetic element into an essentially personal process. This is why words like 'manufacturing' and 'manipulating' are not just part of a rhetoric of disapproval, but express an essential truth about what is being done. To be a parent is to create in one's own image, from one's own flesh and blood. I know that in some cases this is not possible, but I am not here and now concerned with what might be necessary to have a child at all. My concern is with the deliberate imposition on another human being of innate characteristics selected to fulfil its parents' predilections. In religious terms this smacks more of magic and idolatry than true creation. Magic is the attempt to control what cannot be fully understood. Idolatry is an escape from the reality of what is genuinely other than ourselves, into the self-regarding worship of what our own hands or minds have made. Creation, by contrast, endows another being with freedom to be itself. It is on such grounds as these that the concept of designer babies can be seen to strike at the heart of traditional religious beliefs about what human persons are. This does not imply a static view of human nature. The element of sheer givenness which I have been concerned to defend in no way precludes massive personal and cultural changes in the interests of improving human nature, but the difference between these and genetic manipulation is that they are personal and voluntary. People need to be able to own for themselves their own personal history. An educational programme, for instance, would be condemned if it failed to respect the integrity and personal responsiveness of those being taught. But a scientifically improved embryo is given no such respect as a person. It is merely used as a means to someone else's end. Such use is at present deemed to be tolerable in an experimental context only when the embryo is not subsequently allowed to develop into an individual. Outside such a strictly limited experimental context I do not see how the use of embryos could be justified at all. When the argument is made that designer babies would be 'unnatural' it is this deep feeling of offence against the givenness of the other person which I believe lies at the heart of it.[10]

The fact that many people with disabilities are fiercely antagonistic to the idea of genetic manipulation bears out this point. It is not that they welcome disability, or wish to see it in other people, but that they accept and value their own identity. They also fear that in an 'improved' world they could feel resented for being what they are, and their parents could be blamed for allowing them to exist in the first place. While it is usually possible to defend a particular act of selection or interference on the grounds that exceptional individual suffering might be alleviated, the cumulative effect of such actions subtly changes public attitudes. Ultimately at stake, therefore, is the public perception of what human beings are, and the extent to which the natural diversity of an imperfect world is to be welcomed.

By way of postscript to this discussion, it may be useful to take warning from the United States. There are reports that, for some citizens, procreation (I use the word for its deliberate echoes of creation itself) has already been commodified to the point at which it is possible, and legal, to make bids of tens of thousands of dollars on the Internet for the eggs and sperm produced by glamour models. 'We bid for everything else in this society,' said the owner of the website, 'why not eggs?'[11]

GENETICALLY MODIFIED FOODS

I turn now to a further use of genetics among the varying attempts to improve nature – the equally controversial topic of genetically modified foods. Here the ethical issues are quite different. There are no reasonable ethical objections to modifying crops and foods as such. It has always been done. Human survival has depended on it as the world population has increased, and there is an urgent need, particularly in developing countries, for crops which will produce more food in harsher conditions than any of the naturally occurring varieties. I take this as the baseline from which discussion of GM foods has to start. This debate is not about the desires and vanities of human control freaks, as the discussion of cloning and designer babies tends to be, but about human necessities and how the world is to be fed.

The controversies centre on methods, risks, and on how far it is possible to change or accelerate natural processes before they take their revenge on us. There are also highly charged social attitudes towards the idea of genetic modification itself. In the background are enough examples of previous nutritional and ecological disasters using conventional methods, to make one cautious. We live in the post-BSE era.

In the first chapter I mentioned my own involvement in one controversial area where all these factors operate. Preparation for the possible transplantation of animal organs into humans has led to the breeding of thousands of genetically modified pigs. The idea has been to overcome the first and most violent stage of tissue rejection in humans by developing a line of pigs containing the human genes to control this immunological reaction. This has entailed a long breeding programme in which successive generations have been sacrificed. At the time of writing it is an open question whether many more such pigs will continue to be bred, but the feelings likely to be aroused by any proposal to eat them are still worth exploring, if only as an illustration of many people's instantaneous reactions. Such pigs have a much higher standard of cleanliness than ordinary farm pigs. Apart from their cleanliness, they look like ordinary pigs, behave like ordinary pigs, and would no doubt taste like ordinary pigs. But even if it could be demonstrated beyond question that the immunological risks of eating them were insignificant, the chance of humanised pig meat being socially acceptable is nil, no matter how irrational this might appear from a scientific perspective. We share a high proportion of our genes with pigs anyway, and these GM pigs are not remotely human. Nevertheless, what offends is the very idea of them, as does the idea of 'Frankenstein foods'. Both arouse similar emotions, not least because, as I pointed out at the beginning of this chapter, food in human society always carries strong cultural overtones. The growing popularity of organic products testifies to the same rejection of what is felt to be 'unnatural'.

Such feelings apart, what are the actual differences between GM foods and traditional ones? Both have been developed through careful programmes of improvement. The methods differ in that direct genetic modification allows improvements to be more precisely controlled, to take place in much larger leaps, and to use combinations of genes from different species, a leap which would not be possible using conventional methods of breeding. In all three respects genetic improvement can be thought of as scientifically sophisticated, or unnatural – according to taste. As a high-tech operation, requiring massive investment, it also needs to take place on a large scale and to secure global markets, thereby increasing the social risks, should anything go wrong.

Traditional breeding methods, by contrast, seem safer, slower, cheaper, and less effective. They could be described as a form of assisted evolution, in which the selection of natural variants is made by the breeder instead of being left to normal competitive pressures within the environment. But because each step in the process is small, and progress is slow, the usual competitive evolutionary pressures are not entirely absent, with the result that checks and balances are likely to develop alongside humanly contrived adaptations. Nature, in other words, has time to adjust. In addition, since breeding programmes in the past have on the whole been local, the consequences of mistakes are likely to have been local too.

I stress the importance of competitive evolutionary pressures despite the fact that neither form of breeding really takes place on an evolutionary time-scale. The point is that scientifically controlled genetic manipulation propels the creation of new organisms and varieties much further and faster than has ever happened previously, outside the evolutionary framework. It thus places a greater onus on those who undertake it to assess the impact of any new product on the total environment into which it is to be introduced. But such assessment is extremely difficult, and the risks are compounded by the enormous inducements, both humanitarian and commercial, to spread what are hoped to be advantageous developments as widely and quickly as possible.

The public perception that scientists have been moving with unseemly haste in areas they do not fully understand, seems to lie at the heart of worries about the unnaturalness of genetically modified foods and crops. It goes hand in hand with a certain perception of nature as having its own inalienable character. But it is misconceived if the contrast is simply drawn between so-called natural foods and unnatural foods. Almost everything we eat is the result of successive improvements on what nature in the wild originally offered us. The real contrast is between different processes, those in which checks and balances have developed over long periods of trial and error, and new more scientifically based processes in which trust has to be placed in those who tell us that they have foreseen all the problems. Many of the worries are compounded by doubts about how far it is safe to rely on comparatively new knowledge, which has only been tested under laboratory conditions, in a matter as fundamental to us as the food we eat.

In facing these worries it is useful to draw a further distinction between GM foods and GM crops. Products and processes need different kinds of evaluation. A product, being a physical object, can in principle be subjected to rigorous testing and analysis. A process is much more difficult to characterise completely, especially when there is no certainty about where its spatial and temporal boundaries lie.

If a GM food has been produced under controlled conditions, and modified with well-characterised genes, there is in principle no limit to the thoroughness with which it can be analysed for possible toxic side-effects. Claims that GM foods are safe can thus be directly related to the amount of testing which has been done. It is not possible to test, though, for something nobody has thought of. In science, as in life, there is always the unexpected, but this is equally true of traditionally produced foods, as the BSE outbreak and its link with CJD in humans has amply demonstrated. Protagonists of GM foods may justifiably claim that the degree of standardisation involved means that they are probably safer than new varieties of food produced by conventional methods, given that the latter are less easily controlled, and not subjected to the same degree of scrutiny. Against this claim has to be set the difficulty of foreseeing all the possible consequences of some major genetic change, especially when genes from different species are artificially combined. One of the major errors in the early days of GM foods was the failure to anticipate allergic reactions. There was a near disaster from nut allergy, when genes from brazil nuts were used to enhance the nutritional value of soya. Although there are mechanisms in place now to safeguard against such dangers, the multiplication of allergies and the idiosyncrasies of sufferers make this a tricky area to police.

The growing of GM crops gives rise to quite a different set of problems, and I have already hinted at these in my earlier reference to evolutionary checks and balances. The risks do not lie in the crops themselves which, like the foods derived from them, are analysable, and which may well have been designed to cope with the problems of a specific environment, or the needs of a specific population. A rice crop, say, modified to produce Vitamin A could overcome one of the major health problems in many rice-growing areas. Cereals adapted to flourish in dry or salty conditions could prevent famine. Herbicide-resistant crops could enable farmers to wipe out weeds – always provided the farmers themselves are not bankrupted by profitable collusion between the producers of seeds and the producers of herbicides. The potential benefits are huge. The most immediately obvious risks are to the environment, and these are worrying because, unlike possible toxins in foods, they are enormously difficult to identify, assess, and eliminate.

Weed-free crops, for instance, may sound like a good idea. But do we actually want a countryside from which weeds, and all that live on them, have been eliminated? Some parts of the world, no doubt, can thrive on monoculture, where vast prairies are for all effective purposes isolated from the wider environment. But most of the world is not like that. Nature thrives on diversity. It is in small-scale territories like Britain that the risks inherent in the wholesale genetic modification of crops are most apparent. The threat is not so much to people as to the many complex interactions between multiple organisms. It appears all the more pressing because the processes involved, however carefully managed, are in the long run uncontrollable. Nobody can control the flight of pollen, or insects or birds, and in trials undertaken so far there has been no systematic study of the local ecological baselines against which the long-term effects of GM crops need to be measured.

These are familiar criticisms, but I repeat them to make the point that it is not the unnaturalness of GM crops in themselves which is at issue, but our ignorance of their consequences for the environment, together with differing value judgements about the significance of those consequences. There is thus plenty of room for disagreement.

One form this can take centres on the question whether there is, or is not, a so-called 'balance of nature' which ought to be preserved, and which the proliferation of GM crops might disturb. Much of the language about the conservation of nature presupposes that there is such a balance, and in the short term this seems to be so. If there is a fall in the number of larks or thrushes, we assume that something is wrong, and look for an immediate cause in the use of weedkillers or the destruction of hedgerows. And it is surely right that we should take appropriate action. The concept of sustainable development implies that there is something to be sustained, not just for our own immediate benefit or that of our descendants, but out of respect for the long-term stability of particular environments.

Among biologists, though, the belief that there is a stable and continuing balance of nature looks increasingly unlikely, despite continuing interest in the Gaia hypothesis.[12] Though it is possible, even plausible, that the environment of the planet as a whole may be in some measure self-regulating, this cannot rule out major upsets of the kind which have happened in the past, and are likely to happen again, whether or not human beings are to blame for them. On an evolutionary timescale nature seems to lurch like a drunk from one form of temporary balance to another. Species flourish or decay, weather patterns fluctuate, the struggle for survival takes a different turn, and life adapts itself to new circumstances in a dynamic ever-changing system in which the majority of species have already become extinct. Far from there being a natural balance, life represents a constantly shifting pattern in response to repeated threats and opportunities. No species, including ourselves, has an absolute right to survive. While it may be wise, therefore, to set limits on our degree of interference with this system for a variety of reasons, ranging from our grossly inadequate understanding of it, to fears about our own extinction, there are no purely scientific grounds, it is claimed, for positing some pre-existing balance which supposedly gives absolute protection to the *status quo*.

In short there are good reasons both to be cautious about introducing unknown factors into this dynamic and potentially unstable system, and also to be bold in trying to take effective control of those aspects of it which have prime significance for human life. The arguments between cautious conservationists and adventurous innovators are set to continue, as are questions about how to balance concern for our own species with respectful care for the natural world as a whole. In the specific matter of GM crops there remains much which could be done on a purely scientific level to reduce the risk of unwanted side effects.

One of the more exciting possibilities involves research on a method which could enable hybrid crops to breed true. Many of the best strains are hybrids, but the seeds they produce, on the whole, are not; rather than breeding hybrids, they tend to revert to the original strains from which the hybrid was made. The consequence is that new hybrid seeds have to be bought every year. Some plants, however, can be taught to clone themselves, and at the same time to dispense with accepting or producing pollen. GM plants with this property would have the double advantage of not being able to transfer genes via pollen to other plants, and of enabling farmers to take their hybrid seeds direct from last year's crop. At present these are hopes rather than actualities, but if as seems likely they come to fruition, they will remove two of the most telling objections to GM crops, the fear of genetic contamination, and financial domination by the big seed producers. They will not, however, do anything for the maintenance of genetic diversity. Rather, the reverse, and this remains a worry about all successful revolutionary products likely to sweep the market.[13]

This latter point is a reminder that not all problems are scientific, or capable of being solved by ingenious scientific advances. In the previous section on the genetic modification of human beings, I appealed in the end to a set of values about the nature of persons, values which have complex roots in the respect for human life and individuality, the need for social arrangements which validate human diversity, and religious insights into what human beings essentially are and can become. Similar considerations ought to weigh heavily in attitudes towards GM agriculture.

It is perhaps significant that some of the earliest protests about what was happening came from bodies primarily concerned with social justice towards developing countries. As long ago as 1979 questions about genetic engineering were on the agenda of the World Council of Churches.[14] By 1982 a WCC report was criticising the role of major seed suppliers in trying to patent new hybrids for world-wide distribution, and was urging third world countries to protect their own genetic resources. I am not claiming that the WCC had a monopoly of such concerns, but as I was heavily involved in these discussions throughout the 1980s, I can testify at first hand that it was the social implications of GM crops which at that early stage dominated the agenda. It is not surprising, therefore, that the present eruption of public concern was triggered by a new gene which could have had massive social consequences.

Monsanto's 'Terminator' gene was a brilliant conception. If there are worries about the spread of new genes to unmodified crops where they are not wanted, why not arrange for a GM plant to sterilise its seeds after it is fully grown? At a stroke one of the main environmental objections to GM crops is removed. Unwanted genetic side effects could not proliferate. Furthermore Monsanto would reap the added benefit of forcing farmers to buy next year's seed from them as well. What they left out of their calculations was the devastating effect this would have on the poorest parts of the world, the very places where plants able to cope with harsher environments are most needed. This was in 1998, and it marked the beginning of widespread public protest.

Less dramatic, but of greater long-term significance, are the continuing debates about how effectively developing countries can actually use GM crops. There are those who see them as the key to salvation from poverty, provided the technology can be tailored to suit the needs of particular cultures and environments. Some notable successes, backed up by good educational pro-grammes, have transformed areas previously dependent on subsistence agriculture. But it is clear that even the use of suppos-edly safe pesticides in some areas is fraught with difficulties. The World Health Organisation estimates that in the world's poorest countries between two and five million people are poisoned by pesticides each year, 40,000 of them fatally.[15] GM crops against this backcloth of misuse could be a recipe for disaster. As a contrast to these gloomy prognostications, there are reports of experiments in East Africa, in which weeds planted among the maize have cut out the need for pesticides altogether. The local pests seem to prefer eating the weeds. Suitable weeds can also provide a supply of nitrogen from the atmosphere, thus elimina-ting the need for nitrogen-based fertilisers. It is claimed that by the use of such low-tech methods crop yields in the poorest farms have increased by an average of 73 per cent.[16] It would be a pity, therefore, if such simple solutions to some of the problems of subsistence agriculture, tailored to the culture of the people concerned, were to be overlooked in the rush to promote highly sophisticated improvements, which would also make them dependent on resources far beyond their own control. Memories of the Green Revolution, and its long-term legacy of depleted soil and water resources, lead some to question whether further advances down a similar route can actually be sustained.

I am not qualified to judge, but the existence of the debate is itself evidence that in our dealings with the natural world, scientific, social, and historical factors all have relevance. What people are willing to accept as improvements on nature is relative to their particular way of life. The whole subject also raises fundamental questions about how far the impetus to improve depends on beliefs about what nature is, what its possibilities are, and about our own place within it.

WHY IMPROVE?

I suggested at the beginning of this chapter that human beings are inveterate improvers, despite an exceedingly slow start. But though there are basic human skills and desires which seem to be universal, there have in practice been enormous differences in human achievements in different cultures and at different stages of development, and in the conscious motives which have inspired them.

Circumstances obviously play a part in these differences. In a study of transition from a nomadic to a settled way of life in the early history of India,[17] the point is made that nomads in equilibrium with their food supply, tend not to look for much improvement in their way of life. Similarly a settled agricultural community with just enough food, is likely to be cautious about changing anything for fear of upsetting a delicate balance. But an agricultural community which is able to colonise new land where resources are plentiful, is likely to begin thinking of itself as separate from nature, and hence as possessing a right to exploit it for its own ends. The impetus, or lack of it, in this kind of primitive society, to improve on what nature provides, seems to depend on an awareness of natural abundance, of possibilities which have hitherto been unimaginable, because life has been too preoccupied with the business of surviving. And this in turn can lead to a different perception of what nature is, and how to relate to it.

Circumstances which allow scope for the imagination are thus one part of the picture, and a philosophy of life which can reckon with the possibility of change, and inspire hopes of fulfilment, is another. A fatalistic or deterministic philosophy cannot realistically look for improvement – only for endurance. Many Christians have felt in the past, and still feel, that any attempt to improve by scientific means on God's creation, must be in some degree blasphemous. Aristotle's view of nature as inherently goal-directed, on the other hand, could be the basis of an intense striving after perfection, but it faced problems of a different kind. A way of life which is possible only in a society not all of whose members can share it, such as that enjoyed by full citizens in ancient Greece, cannot provide the ultimate fulfilment of human nature. This, as we have seen, is a problem with all so-called improvements, in that they immediately raise questions about who controls them and who benefits.

Yet the power to see visions, and to dream dreams, and to strive for excellence, is not in itself vitiated by such practical problems, and has a necessary place in a theology of creation which takes human participation seriously. The frequent accusation that attempts to improve nature are a form of 'playing God' is theologically inept. There is certainly a recurring temptation to overreach our powers for selfish ends, but for those said to be 'made in the image of God' there is also the opposite temptation – to bury our talents for improvement unused and unincreased.[18] Christian hopes about the 'one far-off event, to which the whole creation moves',[19] suggest that from God's perspective time makes a difference, and that believers should therefore be intent on employing it creatively.

The themes I have been exploring in this book all imply attitudes towards the natural world which assume that improvement is possible. Nature is to be understood in order to realise its potentialities. The respect shown for it by those who created our landscapes was compatible with a subtle discovery and drawing out of its capabilities.[20] The beauty we value, not least in the exotic variety of flowers, owes much to human art and artifice. Even modern attempts to improve the fundamental constitution of living things, as in genetic engineering, have their parallel in the quasi-religious attempts by the alchemists to do the same with matter. They were inspired, as one of them claimed, by 'many irrefutable and uncontestable testimonies that nature itself procreates and prepares seed-bearing creatures whereas the art [of alchemy] works together with them towards the end which nature creates'.[21]

Individuals, too, often dream about, and frequently strive after, some kind of excellence, beating their 'personal best', not only in sport but in all fields of human activity. Even the use of consciousness-enhancing drugs is additional, rather sad, evidence of the widespread human desire for self-transcendence. It is not surprising, therefore, that thoughts about improving nature, and the restless longings which inspire it, should lead eventually to questions about nature's God.

SIX

NATURE'S GOD

'Salad's on a new footing now, apparently,' Mam said, looking at her copy of *Ideal Home*. 'It doesn't just have to be lettuce and tomato and a slice of boiled egg. They eat celery with apple now and you can put raisins in if you want. All the boundaries are coming down.'[1]

So began one of Alan Bennett's incomparable monologues. And of such small things as his Mam observed are revolutions made. Raisins in salads in Leeds in the 1950s were ominous signs of things to come. It would be smorgasbord next. And it is not only in food that the boundaries have come tumbling down. We live in a world of almost infinite choice, change and variety, much of it nowadays as transient as *nouvelle cuisine*, a modish triumph of style over substance.

In the previous chapters I have been attempting to map some of the changing boundaries within the concept of nature. It has a complex history, so complex and so heavily flavoured by cultural seasoning that, though we cannot do without it, the word might almost serve as a recipe for confusion. Nature as studied by the natural sciences, for example, is not the same as the nature which the conservationist wishes to preserve. To behave naturally does not mean the same as obeying natural law. Nature has been externalised as that which stands over against us human beings, needing to be conquered and brought under control, yet at the same time we ourselves are inextricably part of it.

One way of throwing light on this complexity is to list some of the concepts with which nature has been contrasted. For instance, there is a range of opposites centring round the concept of the 'artificial' – constructed, developed, interfered with, urbanised, genetically modified – all of which imply some kind of change induced by human beings in what originally was simply *there*, given in the nature of things. Implicit in these meanings is the supposed dichotomy between nature and culture, rapidly becoming more problematic the more it is studied. A different sort of contrast is to be found in the word 'unnatural'. This has a narrower meaning, often with strong moral connotations. Unnatural behaviour implies some sort of violation of the way things should be. 'Non-natural', on the other hand, occurs only in philosophy, and refers to abstract qualities, such as goodness, which lie outside the purview of the natural sciences. Naturalistic philosophers doubt whether there are any. 'Supernatural' also refers to what lies beyond the study of the natural, but in a theological rather than a philosophical context, and is thus even more suspect in the eyes of naturalism. In popular usage it has strong overtones of strangeness, abnormality or spookiness. There is also nature as contrasted with grace, to which I shall be returning at the end of this chapter.

A common thread running through all these contrasts is that they represent a departure from some kind of normality. Despite its variety of uses and its potential for misunderstanding, the concept of nature seems to do its work by pointing to a quality of givenness, whether in the way things are, the way they used to be, or the way they ought to be. It is a quality I have already referred to more than once, and might seem the obvious basis from which to begin an exploration of what could be meant by 'nature's God'. Religious believers have frequently regarded one of the functions of religion as being to protect and preserve the boundaries of what is held to be natural, given in the act of creation itself. Traditional religion is about order, discipline, direction, the unchanging reality at the heart of things. In an age when all the boundaries are coming down, this sense of an ultimate givenness is all the more precious, and it is not surprising that many traditional believers should feel that the world as they conceive it, and they themselves, are under threat.

Karen Armstrong in her study of fundamentalisms has provided a graphic account of the fear and anger induced in communities which have found their religious environment being destroyed and drained of meaning. In many parts of the world the violent reactions provoked by secularism have confounded all expectations about the gradual erosion of religion. But she has also pointed out the paradox that in trying to counteract the erosions of secular society and fill the resulting void, the various fundamentalisms have inadvertently created something new. 'It is important to realise,' she writes, 'that these movements are not an archaic throwback to the past; they are modern, innovative and modernising.'[2] At the heart of their reaction has been the translation of what was once regarded as mystical and unsayable, into a dangerously inward-looking and quasi-scientific literalism. a reaction to the Enlightenment.

This newness is itself a sign of life, however misguided it might be in these particular instances. Within any lively religious faith the readiness to respond to challenge and to venture into new territory is a necessary complement to order, discipline, and direction. Belief in God has again and again led to the breaking of boundaries, to the unleashing of energy, to outbursts of creativity. There can be fiercely critical elements within faith, sometimes directed outwards against 'enemies' as in the fundamentalisms, but often more constructively directed inwards towards the further exploration of faith itself. To applaud such breaking of boundaries is not to deny a basic God-given order in the way things are. It is to recognise that within the way things are, there is also huge unrealised potential.

What is true of religion is equally true of nature. By itself givenness is too static a quality to convey the dynamism inherent in nature as commonly experienced, not least when it is encountered as the untamed forces of nature. A rough sea impresses us by its unpredictability, its lack of order, its potential for destruction. Evolution impresses by its creative potential, but like the sea it has no predetermined goal. In its most comprehensive sense nature is not a thing, but a system, a vast bundle of possibilities. The earliest meaning of the word referred, not only to the character and being of things, but also to their being born (*natus*), what they were for, and what they might become. This sense of 'becoming' tended to be ignored both when theologians envisaged nature in its present form as a once-for-all creation by God, and when the scientific image of nature as a vast predetermined machine was in the ascendant. Nowadays we know that that machine was no more than a convenient human construct, a way of describing the world which highlighted its static and machine-like properties. The natural world, as we now understand it, is one long history of change, and seems almost infinitely adaptable. The leading spirits of our age look more to the future than to the past. As we saw in the previous chapter, it is what we have the power to do to nature, which now arouses most excitement and opposition. Indeed some scientists, prophets, and planners are so ready to dream of what might be, that there is a danger of losing a sense of the sheerly given, and of our human limitations in the face of it.

Both insights are needed, givenness and potentiality. The concept of nature, with all its variability and ambivalences, forms a seamless web. In what follows I shall seek to spell out further how these ambivalences have their counterparts and correlations within religion, and in particular within a Christian understanding of nature's God.

KNOWING MORE THAN WE CAN PROVE

By the 'givenness' of nature I mean more than the given character of material reality, though that is certainly part of what is meant. The world is what it is, and matter is its most obvious manifestation. But we can also discern laws of nature, and these too seem to have a quality of givenness. Though their form depends heavily on concepts we have ourselves invented, they truly represent something of enduring and practical significance in our dealings with day to day phenomena. It is a fashionable conceit of extreme postmodernism to suppose that our perceptions of the world are so individual, and so culturally conditioned, that we are all the time creating our own reality. I see this as a form of *nouvelle cuisine* for the jaded mind. Nobody believes it when they get into a car, or want a sustaining meal, or step out of a second storey window. There are constants within our experience on which we have to rely as a basic condition of being alive at all, and there are uncomfortable reminders that reality has a character of its own when it is too blatantly disregarded. Environmental disasters are part of the price paid for underestimating the complex character of the givenness of the natural world. More controversially, I have put forward earlier in these pages the case for a kind of moral givenness, in the sense that there are some values so basic that our being human depends on them. The high values placed on life, knowledge and sociability are perhaps the clearest examples.

Alongside these given elements in everyone's experience, most people are also aware of the huge capacity for change, development, growth, exploration, creativity, both in specifically human matters and in the natural world itself. Some of this found expression in Romanticism, in its revolt against mechanism and rationalism. But it was Darwin who gave the concept of potentiality its modern form and significance. Evolution is not just a biological theory. It has become one of the key categories for understanding almost every aspect of our changing experience. For many conservative religious believers it has also been a main cause of the alarm and counter-reactions described earlier in this chapter. It is said that 47 per cent of all US citizens and a quarter of all their college graduates, reject even the basic scientific theory.[3] Nor is this just an American phenomenon. A recent survey of first-year biology and medical students in Glasgow University revealed a rejection rate of around 10 per cent.[4] Whatever doubts some might have about the means by which evolution takes place, however, there is nothing specifically irreligious in the idea of creation as gradually revealing its potential. Indeed the progressive unfolding of potential is inherent in the biblical understanding of history. The relevant theological concepts are 'hope' and 'promise'.

But this is to anticipate. For the moment I am concerned with both givenness and potentiality as belonging firmly within a scientific understanding of the material world. Their relationship can be expressed in the concept of matter as composed of a limited number of particles, forces, states, or whatever, which can interact and be combined in an almost limitless number of ways. These ultimate constituents are simply given. But there remain unresolved questions about the basis and true nature of this givenness, and it is difficult to see how there could ever be any final answer to them. Supposedly final answers to questions about what these ultimate constituents are, and where they came from, always in practice presuppose some prior reality, even if it is only the laws according to which such a prior reality can manifest itself. If, as some cosmologists now tell us, the universe began with quantum fluctuations in a vacuum, there are still questions to be asked about how what purports to be nothing, can have such strange properties as to generate a universe or, as some think, an infinity of universes. No matter how far successive layers of explanation may take us, there always seems to be an indissoluble residue of givenness.

The fact that we can puzzle over such conundrums raises similarly intractable problems about ourselves. How is it that we can know these things? And if the cosmologists and physicists really are disclosing to us the ultimate nature of reality, how can knowledge about this world of particles and forces ever be adequate to account for our subjective experience which, like the particles themselves or their precursors, shares the quality of simple givenness. Yet it is out of this rich mix of different kinds of knowledge that the whole world as we know it, in all its incredible complexity, and with huge potential still untapped, can in theory be constructed.

It would be tempting at this point to conclude that the intractability of these problems is evidence that science needs to be supplemented by religion. The ultimate basis of givenness must transcend the world of material phenomena. But this is not a step which scientists can validly take – as scientists. Specifically theological explanations, it is claimed, must be rigorously excluded from the scientific agenda on the grounds that they have no explanatory value. There is no way in which they could be tested, and in the eyes of the majority of scientists they have the malign effect of stopping further scientific investigation. If God is the answer to a scientific question, there is no more which can be said, because God is by definition the point at which all explanation ends. There is thus a strong motive for treating the scientific world of givenness and potentiality as self-sufficient, despite the unanswered questions about its ultimate basis.

From a theological perspective, too, it is wise to be cautious about any attempt to use theology to supplement science. A Gifford lecturer cannot but be aware of the long history of failed attempts to prove the existence of God from some scientific starting point.[5] The inherent problem in all such attempts at proof is how an argument which begins from the study of the natural world, can rise above its source to demonstrate by reason what must lie beyond both reason and nature. Unless God is in some way already known, perhaps through a sense of wonder, perhaps through personal experience within a religious tradition, perhaps as the answer to an intolerable absence of meaning, or perhaps simply in our puzzling about our own subjectivity, the act of recognition that this is God, or that is his handiwork, cannot be made. It is a common feature of the experience of religious conversion to describe it, not as finding God, but as being found by one whose presence has already made itself obscurely apparent.

A late comment by Wittgenstein echoes the experience of many believers:

> A proof of God ought really to be something by means of which you can convince yourself of God's existence. But I think that *believers* who offered such proofs wanted to analyse and make a case for their 'belief' with their intellect, although they themselves would never have arrived at belief by way of such proofs. 'Convincing someone of God's existence' is something you might do by means of a certain upbringing, shaping his life in such and such a way.

Life can educate you to 'believing in God'. And *experiences* too are what do this but not visions, or other sense experiences, which show us the 'existence of this being', but e.g. sufferings of various sorts. And they do not show us God as a sense experience does an object, nor do they give rise to *conjectures* about him. Experiences, thoughts – life can force this concept on us. So perhaps it is similar to the concept 'object'.[6]

It is instructive to compare the role given to formal proof in that statement, with the classic metaphysical proofs of the existence of God as set out by St Thomas Aquinas. They might seem to be worlds apart, and in their form they certainly are. But even in St Thomas there is an explicit recognition that metaphysical argument by itself cannot do the job, without some prior knowledge of the God towards whom the argument leads. As Paul Tillich once put it, '. . . the religious Ultimate is presupposed in every philosophical question, including the question of God. *God is the presupposition of the question of God.*'[7] In line with this, each of St Thomas's proofs ends with the claim 'and all call this being God'. The argument from causality, for instance, can do no more than point to a first cause, and thus to the dependence of all things on an ultimate originator. But this philosophical abstraction is a long way from the apprehension of God to which believers actually respond. In so far as the proofs worked at all, they drew attention to the implicit presence of God in certain general categories of human experience such as causality, contingency, valuation, and purpose. The argument that all these pointed beyond themselves to some transcendent reality was an admission that they were not self-explanatory. In fact the whole attempt to argue in this way amounted to an exposure of the limits of metaphysical reasoning, though that is not how the arguments were understood at the time. In our own day when, thanks among others to Wittgenstein himself, the limitations of metaphysical reasoning are more readily acknowledged, they can be seen as paving the way for what Karl Rahner described as 'man's basic and original orientation towards absolute mystery, which constitutes his fundamental experience of God'.[8] The arguments could thus give an insight into part of what is meant by the knowledge of God, without themselves constituting wholly rational proofs.

The difference between proving God's existence and recognising it is fundamental. A proof of God's existence would implicitly claim such a knowledge of God's necessary being as to put the author of the proof in a quasi-godlike role. This has not deterred some believers from making the claim, and telling the rest of us in great detail exactly what God is like. To recognise God, though, entails no such claim. Recognition is made up of glimpses here and there, flashes of insight, the making of connections, life itself and suffering, and the gradual refinement of interpreted experience, especially the long historical experience which has been revelatory to previous generations. Recognition has its reflective component. Close attention to, and meditation on, the sheer givennness of our own existence and that of the world, can be a source of wonder which is readily transformed into worship and thanksgiving. There is an affinity between attentive silence before some tremendous manifestation of nature or some great work of art, and the experience of contemplative prayer. The recognition of God also has social and moral components, in fact it entails a whole way of living as being open to the discernment that the basis and ground of all that is, has personal dealings with us. Discussion, argument, historical investigation, have their place in all these activities, but they cannot substitute for what the late Ian Ramsey used to describe as 'the dropping of the penny', 'the dawning of the light', the recognition that this perceived reality is what religion is essentially about.[9] I am reminded of the Chinese proverb, 'Does one light a torch to see the sun?'

To those looking for rational proof of God's existence, or for scientific explanations of how God's activity can be discerned in nature, such an emphasis on recognition might seem like a deliberate evasion of the hard questions. On the contrary, it is an identification of where the hard questions actually lie. There is no independent standpoint, no objective vantage-ground, from which the basis of all reality can be analysed and described. Nor can all our knowledge be sustained by proof. One of the fundamental insights of twentieth-century philosophy can be summed up in the aphorism, 'We know more than we can prove,' a statement which paradoxically is itself capable of logical proof.[10] There is a knowledge which has to precede argument, just as there is a tacit and personal knowledge of language and other skills, which cannot be translated into some more fundamental form, capable of being communicated inter-subjectively. For a rather trivial example of how impossible such translation is, it is only necessary to read an expert trying to describe a wine, as in this actual example, 'brooding with dense smoky richness, whole spice rack in palate ... creamy viscous palate, finishes with opulent savouriness'. In the end there is no way of knowing what a wine really tastes like, except by tasting it.

It is the same lesson the Psalmist had well learned, who wrote, 'Taste and see that the Lord is good.'[11] Words fail us, especially as we try to lay hold on those insights and intimations which make up the experience of God. As Rowan Williams has recently put it, 'It is the theologian's duty to make it difficult for people to speak of God. Genuinely "simple faith" knows this, of course.'[12]

Apart from its theological inevitability, the emphasis on recognition has the further merit of starting with ordinary experience, moral perception, the search for meaning, the encounter with beauty and pain, the awareness of order and chaos, the sense of wonder and shame. These are all matters capable of rational discussion, and are open to illumination and explanation by the various sciences. But they also provide a way into the exploration of a possible spiritual dimension or environment, without foreclosing the question whether such human experience can be truly revealing of God. This starting point in human awareness is in stark contrast to methodologies based on a naturalistic world view from which God is by definition excluded.

Repeatedly throughout this book I have drawn attention to the extent to which our perceptions of nature are culturally conditioned. In the light of this a critic might justly claim that the arguments and insights I have been expressing merely reflect the fact that I am the product of the culture in which I was raised. Indeed my earlier quotation from Wittgenstein gave the game away, in his comment that 'convincing someone of God's existence' might have to entail 'a certain upbringing'. Maybe so. But this is no less true of the natural sciences, whose culture demands a deliberate bracketing out of matters which are seen as belonging within the realm of ethics or aesthetics or personal belief. And rightly so, up to a point, if the natural sciences are to maintain their own integrity. The point at which it ceases to be right is when a scientific world view dismisses, or denigrates, or tries to explain away, aspects of human nature and human experience which have not first been taken seriously in their own terms. The sciences, when they are true to themselves, are not enemies of religion. What is, is scientific imperialism, 'scientism'. Just as neglect of the element of givenness in the natural environment can result in disastrous episodes when nature appears to take its revenge, so scientific projects which are driven ahead in disregard of more subjective human consider-ations, social, ethical and spiritual, can generate a widespread public backlash, based on feelings and insights which have been arbitrarily ignored or disdained. There are already signs of a sad loss of public trust in some forms of science which, while aimed at doing good, create increasing fear and revulsion. It is not just the confusions over BSE, or the violent reactions to GM crops, but the popular worries about what may lie in the future – perhaps ever more dehumanising reproductive techniques, or the limitless horizons for treating human life as manipulable at will, with new threats to distinctive human values.

To perceive the world as a gift of God should in no way inhibit the proper use of scientific knowledge. God is to be understood as the source of nature's potential for change, as well as the source of its fundamental being. The recognition of God as the ultimate giver does, however, make a difference. It entails an acknowledgement of our own creatureliness and responsibility towards what is not ultimately ours. It gives grounds for a basic trust in nature as being hospitable to our needs, to be respected rather than conquered. It affirms our own identity as not needing to prove ourselves over against nature through, for example, over-anxiousness about distinguishing ourselves from other animals, or the self-aggrandisement which would treat all other living things as entirely at our disposal, both of which, sadly, were characteristic attitudes within quite recent times. Neither of them should have any place within a belief in nature as God's creation. Nor, despite the modern growth of so-called earth religions, was it ever necessary to see the world of nature as some kind of rival to God. In Christian belief he is the one who holds it in being, and takes pleasure, not displeasure, in our affection for it, nor does he need it in order to be God. It is the pure gift of love, and we are free to love it because he does, and to develop its potentiality because he has shown his own commitment to time and change by entering into it.[13]

But though God may be recognised as the reality in which nature is grounded, and the source of its potential, he is not the immediate cause of every event. In letting the world be itself, he allows it its own freedom, just as he allows us to be ourselves. This is the meaning of love. To believers in Christ, the self-emptying of God in the Incarnation, his entry into time and change, was not just a temporary episode, but a revelation of how, from the beginning, God has related to his creation. God, as it were, conforms to the self-limitations he has imposed upon himself, in enabling what he has made itself to become creative.[14] A created universe, lacking this element of contingency, would be nothing more than the outworking of a preordained plan, thereby forfeiting all moral significance. It is the relationship between givenness and unconstrained potentiality, as a consequence of God's letting it be, which makes the world the fascinating, glorious, and tragic place it is.

We can see a similar pattern in our own experience of freedom. It is our privilege and responsibility as human beings to go through the long process of creating our own identity. But in creating that identity, we soon encounter the paradox that this is also a process of self-discovery. Our identity as persons is neither given us in advance, nor merely the product of our own actions and interactions with others. We discover that we become most truly and freely ourselves in growing relationship with the one who stands beyond all the competing human pressures on us, as the source of pure gift. To acknowledge the givenness of our nature as a gift of God's love is a basis for ultimate assurance that what we are, and what we may become, really matter. Learning to be a person by fulfilling our potentialities can take place in the confidence that we are already known, and held, and loved by one who does not seek to dominate us by his power, but acts out of sheer gratuitousness.

THE THEOLOGICAL AMBIVALENCE OF NATURE

Sheer loving gratuitousness, however, is not quite so apparent in the world of predators and parasites. Pious sentiments about the glories and beauties of nature cannot hide the cruel reality of many of its aspects. There is a tragic ambivalence in the natural world which poses sharp questions about whether Christians are deceiving themselves in calling it the gift of divine love.

Traditionally this ambivalence has been expressed and explained by describing nature as fallen. The difficulty with this concept of fallenness is that it locates perfection, not in the ultimate fulfilment of creation's potential, but in some golden age in the past, which there are strong reasons to believe never existed. The idea of a golden past may be psychologically real for those who enjoy an emotional after-glow from a happy and innocent childhood, but in a post-Freudian world we are made to look askance even at that. More importantly, a greater historical consciousness, and above all the Darwinian revolution, have changed our way of looking at the world. They have taught us to see nature as a process, not as a finished product. There are, to be sure, elements of human experience which still resonate powerfully with the biblical story of the Fall – the desire to be as gods, the guilt which stems from moral awareness, the sense of exclusion from God's presence, and the inability to know God apart from his own self-disclosure. But the gulf between the world as it is and what love might seem to require, could have an explanation closer to hand if God's mode of creation is through the process of evolution. In a process it is not the beginning but the end which reveals its true character, and if the end is a world made free to make itself, disorder and the suffering that goes with it may be part of the price to be paid.

When Darwin's theory was first propounded some Christians saw the point immediately, and were quick to welcome it as an explanation, both of the apparent wastefulness of creation, and of the otherwise puzzlingly huge variety and fecundity of living things. The theory restored a sense of the natural world as a vast interrelated whole, rather than as a plethora of individually created parts. The more species were discovered, the more absurd it became to imagine each one of them as having been separately designed and created by God. Even creationists these days acknowledge a certain amount of development within the major species. Darwin brought order to what had been growing chaos.

Other Christians, however, while ready to accept the science, have continued to be less sure about Darwinism's theological dividends. They have found it hard to accept the haphazardness of the whole process, the huge extent of the tragedy and waste, and the implication that the underlying law of the universe, far from being gratuitous love, is ruthless competition. Gruesome natural horrors may provide pointed lessons in what a fallen nature might be expected to look like, but how are they to be reconciled with the process of creation by a loving God? Even if we accept that vulnerability and suffering are somehow inherent in love itself, there remains a credibility gap.

The doubts and disagreements still persist, vehemently so as evidenced by the alarming growth of creationism. It is therefore important to be clear about the basis on which the assertion is made that creative love is the ultimate ground of the whole process. It is not an inference from the world of nature itself. Pain, death, competition, and waste were features of the world long before Darwin demonstrated their function. While it is true that he made it easier to see them as necessary, rather than just as brute facts about a world gone wrong, the belief that they are not the final words about life on earth arose long before any such explanations were available. Significantly enough, it arose among a people renowned for their suffering. The Jews have been history's scapegoats. They have survived partly by remembering the past, the givenness, even the arbitrariness, of their call, but also by an unshakeable belief in the future. Their greeting, 'next year in Jerusalem', kept hope alive through long years of exile. God is the God who makes promises, who calls his people into the future, who constantly offers new possibilities, who enables them to live, looking towards what will be, rather than being crushed by what is. It is a faith which in our time barely managed to survive the Holocaust but, strangely, in response to the Holocaust it is now finding a new reason for its own existence, as a warning never to forget the power of evil.

The pattern of promise, suffering, response, and re-creation is reinterpreted in Christianity, with the revolutionary additional insight that it is not only God's people, but God himself who shares the vulnerability of his creation. The whole story of God's 'journey into a far country' is a story of risk, defeat, dereliction, and new life, and it is this which constitutes his greatest gift to us. There is no escaping the horrors of the world, but history has demonstrated again and again that they can be faced, to the extent that God is seen also as the fount of possibility, of hope, and of renewal, the one who draws those who trust him towards an unknown future. I quote Rowan Williams again:

> The 'shape' of Christian faith is the anchoring of our confidence beyond what we do or possess, in the reality of a God who freely gives to those needy enough to ask; a life lived 'away' from a centre in our own innate resourcefulness or meaningfulness, and so a life equipped for question and provisionality in respect of all our moral or spiritual achievement: a life of *repentance in hope*.[16]

A life shot through with provisionality, and lived 'away' from self-sufficiency through 'repentance in hope', necessarily carries with it the risk of loss. It goes against the grain of all those tendencies in human nature which place prime value on security and stability. The Israelites in their desert wanderings wanted to go back to Egypt, where at least they were reasonably safe and well fed, albeit as slaves. Churches can grow comfortable in a state of relative torpor, and quickly disassociate themselves from those who rock the boat. Prophets are without honour in their own country. Yet unless there are those who can unsettle us, shake up our ideas, make us think again, the likelihood is that we shall lose the driving force of faith, the constant reaching out towards a fuller grasp of reality. Danger is the spur to action. Unsettlement is the necessary condition for developing our potential. The first lecture I ever gave, as a young undergraduate, was an early anticipation of this theme. It was on the subject of sleep. I pursued the thesis that sleep is our natural state, and that it is waking which needs to be explained. It was not very good science, but it fitted the condition of my audience, and I think there was a spiritual truth lurking somewhere within it. The aspiration to become what we are not, to rise above our natural state, may need the stimulus of pain, or hunger, or fear, or competition, or just a vivid imagination, but it is the essence of being human, and without it we are couch potatoes.

Can this picture of painful awakening, repentance in hope, and God's promise of things to be, help us to see evolution, and hence nature itself, in a different and more favourable theological light? A theological interpretation of evolution can gain from Darwinism a deeper understanding of how constructive change takes place. It can hold out the hope that suffering is not without an ultimate purpose even though, outside the framework of Christian revelation, this purpose can only be guessed at from insights into human creativity. But there is a need for caution. Too much human suffering has been excused by those perpetrating it on the grounds that they are building a better world. Just as there are moral dangers in being too future-orientated, so there are theological dangers in trying to justify suffering too easily in terms of God's ultimate purposes. Even when this danger is recognised, though, there remains inescapably a kind of suffering, and a necessary ruthlessness, inherent in the process of creation. Teilhard de Chardin memorably described the struggle for life as a process of 'groping':

It means pervading everything so as to try everything, and trying everything so as to find everything. Surely in the last resort it is precisely to develop this procedure that nature has had recourse to profusion.[17]

Within such a process there has to be loss as well as gain, rejection as well as acceptance, death as well as life. What renders it morally bearable from a Christian perspective is the belief that God as Creator and Redeemer endures with us the tragic consequences of a creation which has been dignified by being given its own autonomy. In our own feeble efforts at creativity we can glimpse something of this in our sense of the integrity of the work we undertake, and the pain of all the recalcitrances and rebuffs and rejections involved in producing it. As every budding author knows, two of the most essential pieces of equipment are the waste paper basket and, nowadays, the delete key.

There are ways, then, perhaps only partial and provisional ways, of reconciling the tragic elements of life with belief in some larger providential purpose. What precisely 'providential purpose' might mean has been much disputed by theologians. On the view I have put forward earlier, that God is as self-limiting in relation to the whole of creation as he is self-emptying in the particular events of the Incarnation, we must expect a certain hiddenness. It would be wrong to look for the spectacular exercise of extraordinary divine powers. A self-emptying God could, however, gently guide those attentive and receptive to him towards the fulfilment of his ultimate purposes, and it is not hard to see how openness to God in prayer creates just such an opportunity. Prayer and providence, in fact, have always been closely linked in Christian thought. Belief in providence might also be a way of engaging with those new possibilities and larger horizons opened up by God as the fount of potentiality – a subject to which I shall be returning later in this chapter.

Meanwhile there is a further problem to consider, associated more closely with evolution itself. How is it possible to reconcile belief in providential purpose, and the idea of God as the fount

Does God play dice?

of potentiality for the future, with the scientific orthodoxy that evolution is driven by chance, and is undirected in its outcome?

The reliance on chance is what makes possible de Chardin's vision of evolution as 'trying everything'. The point is that there is no way of knowing in advance what 'everything' entails. The great merit of randomisation is that it is a means of generating hitherto unimagined possibilities by stepping outside strictly logical progression. For this to happen it has to rely on some process, like genetic shuffling, which is inherently unpredictable. A strictly logical progression from one form or idea to another can easily find itself stuck in a groove. A chance event or a random change may spell release. There is an illustration of this in our own mental processes. Simply letting one's mind wander can occasionally generate quite strikingly new thoughts. The trick is to spot them and let them grow, and to weed out what is obviously wrong or unproductive. This is the mental equivalent of natural selection. Randomisation, in other words, can become truly creative, truly serendipitous, when the contingencies it creates are subject to selection in an environment which can distinguish good from bad, well-adapted from ill-adapted. Such selection, as we have seen, necessarily entails loss, just as life entails death. The world is thus inevitably tragic, though not irredeemably so, because without such a process there can be no spontaneous creation. Far from being a theological problem, therefore, chance can be seen as a vital part of the means whereby God allows his creation itself to be creative. To revert to my previous terminology, chance and selection, working themselves out within an appropriate environment, equal evolution, and are a primary means by which the potential inherent in the givenness of things can be released. In this release of new potentialities, the most neglected and, as I now want to suggest, the most theologically significant of these three factors – chance, necessity, and the environment – is the environment.

A MORE COMPREHENSIVE ENVIRONMENT

In biological terms the role of environmental change as a stimulus to evolution is incontestable. Organisms evolve to fit particular ecological niches, and if the niche changes or disappears they have to adapt or die. One has only to think of the extinction of the dinosaurs, and the flowering of new forms of life in their wake, or the extraordinary ability of some bacteria to live in water at a temperature which would kill any other organism. There is also the fact that not all ecological niches are equal, but each imposes its own constraints on organisms and points them towards development in particular directions. Though in theory there are no limits on what might evolve, in practice the physical characteristics of the world make some developments much more likely than others. Giant animals, for instance, have special problems with the force of gravity, which is why they are mostly found in the sea. Two-legged giants would have to have limbs so cumbersome that they would only be able to waddle – like the larger dinosaurs reconstructed by the BBC.

The phenomenon known as 'convergence' is convincing evidence of these environmental constraints. Organisms with very different evolutionary origins can converge towards common shapes or forms in similar environments. Whales, for instance, look like fish because fish have the best shape for living in the sea, but biologically they are totally different. The most famous examples of such convergence are the strong similarities between some placental mammals and their marsupial counterparts, even though their evolutionary lines of descent must have separated from one another somewhere around the Jurassic period.[18] Despite its basis in randomness, therefore, evolution is far from haphazard – a point of some theological interest when one considers how the creation of a universe with particular properties must have far-reaching consequences in terms of what eventually inhabits it. There is the further point that some organisms not only inhabit special ecological niches, they may also modify and adapt them to suit their own way of life. The possession of intelligence is of prime significance in this kind of evolutionary feedback between an organism and its environment, which is one reason for claiming that in one way or another intelligent organisms were bound to appear. For it is not only human beings who gain advantages by creating their own niches. Like somebody building a house, a bird building a well-concealed nest is doing more for the survival of its chicks than one which lays its eggs where any predator can see them. In short, the mutual adaptation between organisms and their environment is a crucial factor in what both eventually become.

But in this fanning out of life to fill all the available niches, where do we draw the line as to what counts as 'environment'? I deliberately use this word, rather than 'nature', because I want to include the possibility that there may be environments which have developmental significance, but which do not fit into the ordinary definitions of nature, protean though we have seen these to be. 'Environment' is a conveniently empty word, despite its strong association nowadays with particular attitudes towards ecological issues. I use it here simply to mean that which environs, surrounds, and supports us, the total context in which our lives are lived. There is our social environment, for example, in addition to our physical environment. Social animals, including ourselves, develop new capacities by virtue of living together and discovering the value of co-operation. Culture as we now know it is the product of this relatively new kind of environment, created no doubt in the first instance out of the necessities for survival, but now enjoyed and valued for its own sake as representing a new level of human existence. May there not also be a spiritual environment, known to us through a dim awareness of what transcends thought and language, a hint of possibilities beyond mutual needs and desires, and a felt pressure to explore what lies beyond? If human beings can indeed recognise and respond to such promptings, this would have profound consequences for what those aware of such a spiritual environment know themselves to be, and seek to become. Its existence might also disclose another dimension in the evolutionary process, whereby the possibilities of receiving some guiding or inspiring or restraining influence from a transcendent reality are part of the total context within which creative development takes place.

This needs careful definition if it is not to seem mere fantasy. I have referred a number of times already to the human impulse to reach out beyond ourselves. Reach out into what? Imagination? That is certainly an important aspect of it, and was the focus of Romanticism's version of what I am attempting to describe. But it is not just imagination as commonly understood, because the whole thrust of such reaching out is that it is perceived to be an encounter with reality, the bringing to consciousness of hitherto unrecognised apprehensions, the discovery of a new depth of meaning, the experience of being drawn towards what is both awesome and fascinating, an uncomfortable awareness of responsibility, an invitation to wake up to our true potential, an acknowledgement of the sacred. There are endless ways of trying to put into words what, in practice, can only be known by experiencing it, but all descriptions include an element of searching within ourselves, as well as a demand from without. These are not marginal human experiences. There is abundant evidence, even in our secular society, that they are widespread, though sadly many of those who have them lack the cultural context in which to make sense of them.[19] To discount such experiences, or turn our backs on them, is to ignore a large part of what makes us distinctively human. To be human is to ask questions, not least about the things which transcend us. To treat such questioning as a means of entry into a new environment which is open to exploration, is to begin to see the natural world as only one aspect of a much larger whole. When that remarkable saint Lady Julian of Norwich famously described the world as 'a little thing, the size of a hazelnut' held in the palm of her hand, in comparison with the sight of her Maker, she wrote as one whose essential life was lived within these larger horizons.[20]

That there is what might be called a 'spiritual or transcendent environment' was the theme of John Oman's great book *The Natural and the Supernatural*. His use of the word 'supernatural' is likely to give the wrong impression today, so debased has the word become by its association with the occult. He meant by it more or less what I have myself tried to express – an environment which impinges on us, with its own peculiar kind of reality, and carries its own assertion of value and significance. In his own words, it is 'the world which manifests more than natural values, the world which has values which stir the sense of the holy and demand to be esteemed as sacred'.[21] In a later passage on what he calls 'the witness of right feeling' to the supernatural, he writes:

> None of the treatises on the sublime and beautiful have in them much to help us, because they are, mostly at least, determined by the rationalist view that everything must be justified by the understanding, whereas all our argument has been that it must be determined by the true nature of our whole environment, and that means by intuition and anticipations which go far beyond what we can set in the clear hard light of the understanding. It concerns primarily what we have suggested about perception, that it is like personal intercourse when speech is more than a set of symbols to be interpreted, something beyond the mere expression of the speaker and the sympathetic response of the hearer, when every word has in it something of the whole mind of the speaker and some direct sense of it in the hearer. It is a judgement of values, but it is what all judgement ought to be, essentially an insight.[22]

In short, just as communication is as much about relationships, as it is about words, so knowledge of the supernatural cannot be reduced to what can be rationally said about it. Just as we can know more than we can prove, so we can experience more than we can describe.

Philosophical fashions have changed, and Oman is almost forgotten. I quote him only as a reminder that the concept of a transcendental environment beyond our physical and cultural environments, has an intellectually respectable history. It is interesting to find it resurfacing in an off-the-cuff remark by a modern Darwinian philosopher in a speculation about what he calls 'zones', where he refers to those who 'have wondered if there might not be another zone beyond culture, for something over and above thinking and intelligence'.[23] The merit of the idea is that it allows a proper place for human spirituality, and does so within a context which is also scientifically credible. The suggestion being made is that reality itself is of such a kind as to be open-ended towards the transcendent. In more familiar theological terms, the world reveals its own createdness, its orientation towards, and its utimate dependence on what lies beyond it, by exposing the limits of our questioning.

Does it follow then that this wider environment is potentially open to other creatures besides human beings? If we take evolution seriously, the answer must surely be yes. True, self-conscious entry into it seems likely to be a distinctive human quality, and to be related to our sophisticated use of language and our degree of self-awareness. Many social animals, though, have rudimentary forms of culture into which their young have to be initiated – the higher primates being the obvious example. Whales also are much given to communication with one another, and there is recent evidence of their ability to learn from different cultures, in that one group appears to be able to pick up another group's songs.[24] But only humans, it seems, have an awareness of the transcendent, and all that follows from it in terms of art, morality, and worship.

Consciousness itself, however, is surely not unique to us, and poses just as many philosophical problems if it is posited in some of the higher animals, as it does when we try to explain it in ourselves. The huge research effort now being devoted to its study will undoubtedly throw more and more light on the brain processes which correlate with it, and the degrees of consciousness to be expected in nervous systems with different degrees of complexity. But the gulf between such objective studies and subjective experience still seems unbridgeable. Perhaps the problem arises because, in the objective study of the natural world, true objectivity can only be attained by setting on one side precisely those aspects of our experience of it which, when developed, emerge as qualities of inwardness, purposefulness, and eventually as conscious thought. However if, as I have suggested earlier, the whole of reality is open-ended towards the transcendent, there is scope for understanding how an increasing degree of inwardness, subjectivity, and ultimately spirituality, might have emerged, as brains evolved which were capable of exploring, responding to, and producing mental representations of this dimension of the total environment. This is not panpsychism, the theory that everything in the universe has an inner or mental aspect. Minds are to be found only where there are nervous systems sufficiently complex to respond, not only to what is immediately present, but to what has been, or might be. Nor am I proposing a disguised form of dualism. There is one reality, but it is a created reality and is therefore capable of disclosing its creator, who is present within it, but hidden, and who as creator transcends it. I am tentatively proposing a theory of the environment, extended to include a spiritual dimension, which can be seen to follow from the belief that all existence is grounded in the reality of God, and thus in the right circumstances can reveal something of its own transcendent source and ground. All existing things can witness to this ground by the givenness of their existence, in that they are what they are by virtue of their relationship with God. Living things can witness, in varying degrees, to God's continuing creativeness, by the emergence of ever-increasing complexity in response to the open-endedness of their environment. Human beings can witness by naming the transcendent, and responding to it as the source and ground of all value.

Against this background it is clear that what we now call nature, or the material world, is a brilliantly successful abstraction, made by deliberately leaving out of account all those dimensions of experience which might serve to reveal this ultimate relationship with its transcendent ground. For many purposes such neglect makes no difference. I have already made the point that the natural sciences only became possible when the ideal of impersonal abstracted knowledge was rigorously pursued. But when we try to understand ourselves and our place within nature, and the moral significance of the processes which brought us into being, or when we try to explain capacities like consciousness which do not fit into a materialistic straitjacket, the neglect of this extended concept of reality becomes serious. It seems folly to discount the only direct knowledge we possess, which is personal, subjective, and shaped by awareness of a mental and spiritual environment incapable of being reduced to something merely physical and external to us.

It is true that this direct experience of ourselves and our world is mediated through culture, and may find differing expression in different contexts. But despite cultural differences we can all recognise something of it in each other and recognise, too, that it points to a reality of supreme value and significance. This is the basis of our respect for other persons. To acknowledge someone as a person is to acknowledge this inwardness, the fact that they belong like us within this larger environment, no matter how deep the gulf may be between us in terms of religion, culture, race, or any other qualities. And it is because the whole of creation shares with us, in greater or lesser degree, this open-endedness towards God, that it too deserves a proper respect and care.

NATURE AND GRACE

I have been exploring the belief that God is both the source of the given character of existence, and the basis of its potentiality for adaptation and change. The theological concept which can hold them together is grace. This has already been hinted in references to the gratuitousness of creation, and to the loving and empowering presence of God which can draw out our potentialities in the continuing process of 'repentance in hope'. The Christian gospel, as the New Testament makes very clear, is the gospel of God's grace, but there are good grounds for thinking that the concept is not unique to Christianity. The other great world faiths may not use the word in the technical sense that Christians use it, but the idea of God as the basis of reality, and the source of unmerited assistance towards the ultimate good, is found in many faiths, among them Judaism, Islam, and various forms of Hinduism. Grace is an important and specific feature of Sikhism. In concentrating on Christian theology in this final section I have no wish to deny the relevance of other faiths to these issues. I do so because I know Christianity from within, and because, for my present purpose in drawing together the different themes of this book, Christian theology can have recourse to a longstanding exploration of the relationship between grace and nature.

One of the more encouraging theological movements in our day has been the growing realisation that grace and nature are not two distinct and separate realities, but much more like two aspects of the same divine gift. When Augustine, in his controversy with Pelagius, wrote about grace that it 'is concerned about the cure, not the constitution of natural functions',[25] he set in train a fateful separation between them. Grace, it was implied, is God's remedy for what has gone wrong, but does not belong to the constitution of nature itself. Even if nature had once been an expression of grace by virtue of its creation, it had lost this in the Fall, so much so that the word could now be used to describe the state of sin from which humanity needed to be delivered – 'the natural man'. Reinforcing this separation was Augustine's own definitive experience of conversion, which had highlighted for him the radical insufficiency of his own nature.[26] But even he was not totally negative. Outside his controversy with Pelagius, his theology was actually a great deal more subtle than was suggested by this over-simple assignment of grace entirely to the supernatural infusion of the divine love – as that which alone makes true goodness possible. Nevertheless the effect of his words was to open the way for later generations to think of nature as if it were the opposite of grace. Even the famous formulation that 'grace does not destroy nature, it perfects it', could be read as underscoring the idea that nature is somehow subservient to humanity, through whom alone grace is mediated to it. Against such a background the natural world ceases to have any intrinsic value, apart from its providential usefulness to us. In the extreme form of separation between nature and grace, the human body itself could be seen as belonging to the

[165]

sinful godless part of reality, in need of redemption from its materiality.

But it is at this point that the absurdity of such total separation becomes obvious. Our bodiliness is essential to what we are as human beings. If God's grace is not to be discerned also in the natural world, we ourselves are locked into a fatal dualism which devalues and downgrades a major part of our own human nature, and sets us in a graceless environment. The theologians of the Eastern Church never fell into this trap. They were much more ready to see creation itself as a work of grace, damaged but not totally defaced by the Fall. A modern evolutionary concept of the created world as unfinished, but dynamic and full of potential, would not have seemed foreign to the Cappadocian Fathers. Gregory of Nyssa's philosophy, for instance, was vigorous in its defence of our human freedom to fulfil our potential, a freedom which according to Augustine had virtually been lost, in so far as, without grace, it was not possible to choose well.[27] Compare that with Gregory in his *Oration on Baptism*, where he described 'the river of grace' flowing everywhere, fulfilling all created things, 'unintelligent and intelligent'.[28] Indeed the very existence of the sacraments, whereby natural objects become means of grace, is evidence that nature, far from being alienated from God, is capable of bearing the image of the divine and becoming the medium of communion with the divine.

It is to Karl Rahner in the mid-twentieth century that we owe the most radical rethinking on the whole subject, arising out of his definition of 'created spirit' as characterised by 'its openness to infinite being'.[29] My earlier description of a spiritual environment making its own contribution to evolutionary development, could have been reformulated in very similar theological language. Rahner draws from his definition the implication that actual human nature is

> never 'pure' nature, but nature in a supernatural order, which man (even the unbeliever and the sinner) can never escape from ... We can only fully understand man in his 'undefinable' essence if we see him as...

being already ordered towards, or in some measure attracted and infused by, grace;

> this is his *nature*. His nature is such that its *absolute* fulfil-
> ment comes through grace, and so nature *of itself* must
> reckon with the *meaningful* possibility of remaining without
> absolute fulfilment.

In other words nature and grace are but two sides of a relationship with the God from whom both derive, and on whom both
depend. That we are by nature capable of responding to God,
and by grace called upon and enabled to do so, does not, of
course, destroy our freedom to refuse. Nevertheless refusal is in
a profound sense unnatural, in that it constitutes a denial of
what being fully human ultimately entails.

If this is true of us as human beings, what are its implications
for nature in its wider aspects? Does it make sense to think of
nature, distinct from human beings, as 'already ordered towards
grace'? There are well-recognised dangers in pressing the analogy
with human nature too far. Organic conceptions of nature have
a long and chequered history. In Chapter 3 I referred critically
to Baalism as one example. An organic interpretation of nature
was, of course, fundamental to Aristotle. There are residues of
organic thinking in the New Testament, in references to mysterious and untameable energies which can generate fear and
subservience. These are the 'cosmic powers ... authorities and
potentates of this dark age ... superhuman forces of evil in the
heavenly realms',[30] from which Christ has delivered us. It is a
way of thinking which resurfaced, with new magical and religious
overtones, during the Renaissance, as part of the reaction against
the increasingly successful mechanical and mathematical models
of the universe.[31] It finds expression today in various forms of
New Ageism as they attempt to tap into 'natural powers'.

The gospel promise is that these potentially dark and
dangerous energies have been overcome, and that no matter how
threatening the powers of nature may seem, they are in the end
dependent on, and subject to, the one gracious God. The growth
of science has in its own way helped to fulfil this promise by

progressively undermining the organic interpretation of nature, and by thus distancing the understanding of how things actually work from the potentially malign influence of spiritual powers. There remain, of course, legitimate fears about natural disasters in a world where the price of creative change, whether the product of evolution or of human contrivance, is a certain basic instability, an element of the unknown and the unpredictable. Yet in many aspects of life there has been a release from the more primitive fears, a mastery of natural forces, and successful measures to cope, at least to some degree, with the otherwise uncontrollable. All of these can on one level be celebrated as human achievements, but it is important to remember that they all at one time had to be grounded in the belief that it is dependable unity, rather than chaos, which lies at the heart of things. In Christian theology it is the world's createdness which is the guarantee of its dependability and regularity, and there are good reasons for thinking that it was this belief which provided the necessary context for the birth of modern science.[32]

Yet just as Israelite religion could not distance itself totally from an immanent organic view of nature, so in today's world, as I have briefly indicated, the belief that God not only transcends nature but is also in some sense present within it, refuses to disappear entirely.[33] What I have called the 'spiritual environment' is one way of describing this divine immanence. Transcendence needs, as it were, to have a foothold in created reality, to be a vital dimension of it, if subjectivity is to be possible, and if creation is to give rise to beings like ourselves who can in some measure understand it. To see in nature the mind of God ordering all things with external mechanical inflexibility would be to concentrate solely on its givenness, and to ignore the sheer limitless potential of the whole enterprise which, from our perspective, appears as gratuitous empowerment from within. In short, it is not only human nature, but nature in its wholeness, which is 'ordered towards grace', a grace which naturally belongs to it.

We need to reckon, though, with the fact that human beings are a very small part of a very large universe. We do not know

whether we are the only beings who can to some extent understand it and perceive its spiritual dimension. To recognise that
gratuitous empowerment need not be limited to us can pro-
foundly change the way we perceive, and behave towards, the
rest of the natural world. It would be very small-minded to
suppose that the gracious love of God which can redeem and
fulfil our own nature is irrelevant to nature at large, just as it
would be to suppose that the wider environment in which we
are called to live our lives, is significant only to us. That God
communicates himself in love through the whole of existence, is
one of the truths to which the Incarnation bears witness. Nature
and grace, on this understanding, both belong within the same
creative outpouring. It follows that the grace encountered in
nature is not a series of occasional special benevolences towards
us, but is the love which draws the whole creation towards its
ultimate fulfilment in God himself. Thus to those who ask, why
should we care about what happens to the world of nature,
except for our own selfish ends? the answer is plain. Nature was
not created for us alone. We may have gained unique powers,
but other forms of existence also have their place within the
purposes of God, a place which has often been shamefully dismissed. To perceive God's graciousness in nature is to see the
world in a new light, and to bring to it a new degree of penitence
and hopefulness.

It is to pause, and to ponder, and to re-order our values, as
the poet R. S. Thomas once lamented his failure to do at the
sight of the sun shining on a bright field.

> I have seen the sun break through
> to illuminate a small field
> for a while, and gone my way
> and forgotten it. But that was the pearl
> of great price, the one field that had
> the treasure in it. I realize now
> that I must give all I have
> to possess it. Life is not hurrying

on to a receding future, nor hankering after
an imagined past. It is the turning
aside like Moses to the miracle
of the lit bush, to a brightness
that seemed as transitory as your youth
once, but is the eternity that awaits you.[34]

NOTES

INTRODUCTION
1. *Humanity, Environment and God*, edited by Neil Spurway (Blackwell, 1993). My own contribution, 'Is There Reliable Knowledge about God?' has been reprinted in John Habgood, *Faith and Uncertainty* (Darton, Longman and Todd, 1997).
2. William Temple, *Nature, Man and God* (Macmillan, 1934).
3. ibid. p. 134.
4. Mary Midgley, *Utopias, Dolphins and Computers. Problems of Philosophical Plumbing* (Routledge, 1996).

Chapter 1: WORDS AND THINGS
1. The three areas of meaning discussed in this chapter correspond to those identified by Raymond Williams in *Keywords* (Fontana, 1976). C. S. Lewis has a rather different classification in *Studies in Words* (Cambridge University Press, 1961). His main interest was in the many different nuances of meaning in English literature. Among more modern treatments of the subject, to which I owe much, are Kate Soper, *What is Nature?* (Blackwell, 1995), and Phil Macnaughton and John Urry, *Contested Natures* (Sage Publications, 1998).
2. Michael Horace Barnes, *Stages of Thought* (Oxford, 2000) pp. 89–90.
3. Jeremiah Chapter 36 is evidence of written prophecies. Isaiah Chapters 40–55 express what is probably the first fully monotheistic faith. Both belong within this crucial period.
4. *The Meditations of Marcus Aurelius*, Book IX, 1.
5. 'To a Youthful Friend', from *Occasional Pieces*.
6. R. G. Collingwood, *The Idea of Nature* (Oxford, 1945) pp. 29ff. The book is particularly helpful on the Greek origins of the idea.
7. Aristotle, *Generation of Animals*, 741b 13.
8. Aristotle, *Physics*, 193a.
9. ibid. 192b.
10. Listed in Collingwood, op. cit. pp. 80–81.

11. Aristotle, *Parts of Animals*, 641a.
12. ibid. 658b.
13. G. Sommerhoff, *Analytical Biology* (Oxford, 1950) pp. 66–70.
14. Aristotle, *History of Animals*, 561a–562a.
15. Aristotle, *Parts of Animals*, 687a.
16. The famous opening words of the *Tractatus Logico-Philosophicus* (Routledge and Kegan Paul, 1922). They need to be balanced by a very different thought near the end of the book: 'There is indeed the inexpressible. This shows itself; it is the mystical.'
17. Joseph Butler, *Sermon VII*, 16.
18. Charles Dickens, *Bleak House*, Chapter 2.
19. Ronald W. Clark, *Einstein. The Life and Times* (Hodder and Stoughton, 1973) p. 443. See also p. 249.
20. I take a guiding principle from an illuminating comment in Fergus Kerr's *Theology after Wittgenstein* (SPCK, 1997) pp. 104–5.

   Things do not reveal their properties to us as if we were totally passive recipients, with no contribution of our own to make. Nor are we absolutely free to impose whatever grid we like upon the raw data of sensation . . . There is no getting hold of anything in the world except by a move in the network of practices which is the community to which we belong.

21. The name of the committee is the *United Kingdom Xenotransplantation Interim Regulatory Authority*. At the time of writing no xenotransplantation procedures have been authorised within the UK.
22. Keith Thomas, *Man and the Natural World. Changing attitudes in England 1500–1800* (Allen Lane, 1983) p. 39.

Chapter 2: STUDYING NATURE

1. The theme is extensively documented in Adrian Desmond and James Moore's *Darwin* (Michael Joseph, 1991).
2. I owe this point to Martin Rudwick's 1996 Tarner Lectures on *Constructing Geohistory in the Age of Revolution*.
3. From H. C. Beeching's *The Masque of Balliol, c.* 1870.
4. An exception is Hilaire Belloc's:
   These things have never yet been seen,
   But scientists who ought to know
   Tell us that it must be so.
   So let us never never doubt
   What nobody is sure about.
5. Lowes Dickinson, *Religion: A Criticism and a Forecast* (Dent, 1905) p. viii. Quoted by Roger Lloyd in *The Church of England in the Twentieth Century* (Longmans, 1946). It is ironic that at about this time Lenin was rigorously pursuing his disastrous belief that there is indeed a science of human history, Marxism, whose predictions because they are scientific are infallible, and can therefore be used to

justify whatever means are employed to fulfil them. Robert Service, *Lenin* (Macmillan, 2000) p. 193.

6. H. P. Rickman, *Wilhelm Dilthey* (Paul Elek, 1979).

7. F. M. R. Walshe, *Critical Studies in Neurology* (E. & S. Livingstone, 1948) pp. viii–ix.

8. John D. Barrow, *Theories of Everything. The Quest for Ultimate Explanation* (Vintage Edn, 1991). The scientific sections of this chapter owe much to Barrow's exposition.

9. E. O. Wilson, 'Biology and the Social Sciences' in *Zygon*, Sept. 1990, p. 247. The theory is discussed by Philip Hefner in R. M. Richardson and W. J. Wilman's *Religion and Science* (Routledge, 1996) pp. 401ff.

10. Ian Stewart, *Life's Other Secret. The New Mathematics of the Living World* (Allen Lane, 1998).

11. James Gleick, *Chaos. Making a New Science* (Cardinal, 1987). M. M. Waldrop, *Complexity. The Emerging Science at the Edge of Order and Chaos* (Penguin, 1992).

12. Hume's most famous contribution to philosophy was his demonstration that efficient causality cannot be shown to be anything more than regular succession. The idea of a necessary connection between cause and effect exists only in the mind. Kant responded to this latter point by arguing that causality is one of the universal categories through which all phenomena are necessarily perceived.

13. Ronald W. Clark, *Einstein. The Life and Times* (Hodder and Stoughton, 1973) p. 73.

14. *New Scientist*, 23 September 2000, pp. 33–5.

15. Martin Rees, *Just Six Numbers* (Weidenfield and Nicolson, 1999).

16. Barrow, op. cit. p. 89.

17. Arthur O. Lovejoy, *The Great Chain of Being. A Study of the History of an Idea* (Harvard, 1936). Citations are from the Harper Torchbook Edition, 1960.

18. ibid. p. 229.

19. ibid. p. 179.

20. Herbert Dingle was at one time Professor of History and Philosophy of Science in the University of London. He published his question, and the story of his many attempts to find an answer to it, in *Science at the Crossroads* (Martin Brian and O'Keefe, 1972).

21. There is a hint of what was later to become an obsession in Sir Arthur Eddington's 1927 Gifford Lectures, *The Nature of the Physical World* (Cambridge, 1928) pp. 243–4:

> ... a strictly quantitative science can arise from a basis which is purely qualitative ... the laws which we have hitherto regarded as the most typical natural laws are of the nature of truisms ... the mind by its selective power fitted the processes of Nature into a frame of law of a pattern largely of its own choosing; and in the

discovery of this pattern of law the mind may be regarded as regaining from Nature that which the mind has put into Nature.

22. Barnes, op. cit. p. 38.

23. Charles Seife, *Zero: The Biography of a Dangerous Idea* (Souvenir Press, 2000). An entertaining and informative book, but spoilt by a highly tendentious reinterpretation of church history.

24. Robert Temple, *The Genius of China* (Prion, 1998) pp. 139ff. The book is a merciful distillation of Joseph Needham's vast series of volumes on *Science and Civilization in China*.

25. Quoted by R. G. Collingwood, *The Idea of Nature* (Oxford, 1945) p. 102.

26. In his early years Bertrand Russell was fascinated by mathematics which he saw as providing our only human access to what is absolute and eternal. Wittgenstein, who was eventually to disillusion him, described mathematics as no more than a technique. The story of their relationship is to be found in Ray Monk, *Bertrand Russell. The Spirit of Solitude* (Vintage, 1997).

27. Barrow, op. cit. Chapter 9 *passim*.

28. The point is that the weather is affected by virtually everything, including itself. This self-reflexiveness enables small causes to have large and distant consequences – the famous butterfly effect.

29. R. A. Fisher, *The Genetical Theory of Natural Selection* (Oxford, 1930). This was a key text in the application of Mendelian genetics to Darwin's theory, which then enabled natural selection to be put on a statistical basis.

30. In *Principia Mathematica*, written in collaboration with A. N. White-head. The story is told in Monk, op. cit., and also more accessibly in Ray Monk and Frederic Raphael (eds.), *The Great Philosophers* (Weidenfield and Nicolson, 2000) pp. 259–91.

31. Gödel's theorem arises out of the kind of logical puzzles which can occur when sentences refer to themselves, e.g. is a Cretan lying when he says 'All Cretans are liars'? If he is, then he isn't, but if he isn't, then he is. Similar things happen when a logical system, like mathematics, seeks to provide logical justification for itself. A formal statement of Gödel's theorem might be 'All consistent axiomatic formulations of number theory include undecidable propositions.' One of its implications is that not everything that is true can be proved. See Douglas R. Hofstadter, *Gödel, Escher, Bach: an Eternal Golden Braid* (Penguin, 1979) p. 17.

32. G. H. Hardy's *A Mathematician's Apology* (Cambridge, 1940) is a classic and very readable statement of this point of view.

33. Simon Singh, *Fermat's Last Theorem* (Fourth Estate, 1997).

34. Barrow, op. cit. p. 101.

35. Quoted in Arthur Gibson, *God and the Universe* (Routledge, 2000) p. 92.

36. The Epilogue to Alan Sokal and Jean Bricmont's *Intellectual Impostures* (Profile Books, 1998) is a vigorous example of this kind of rejection, with the fire mainly directed towards leading French postmodernists.
37. Thomas S. Kuhn, *The Structure of Scientific Revolutions* (Chicago, 1962).
38. Wittgenstein's famous description of different 'language games' must bear some responsibility for this. George A. Lindbeck's *The Nature of Doctrine. Religion and Theology in a Postliberal Age* (SPCK, 1984) is a much discussed example of this tendency. A more recent example, this time from the scientific side, is Stephen Jay Gould's *Rocks of Ages: Science and Religion in the Fullness of Life* (Jonathan Cape, 2000).
39. J. Wentzel van Huyssteen, *The Shaping of Rationality. Towards Interdisciplinarity in Theology and Science* (Eerdmans, 1999) p. 49.
40. Barnes, op. cit. p. 187.
41. Karl R. Popper, *Objective Knowledge. An Evolutionary Approach* (Clarendon Press, 1972).
42. Barbara Herrnstein Smith, *Belief and Resistance. Dynamics of Contemporary Intellectual Controversy* (Harvard, 1997) pp. 139–40.
43. *New Scientist*, 17 February 2001, pp. 26–30. The article is a summary of a paper by Anton Zeilinger on 'A Foundational Principle for Quantum Mechanics'. The following quotation captures the gist of it:
    Because we can only interrogate nature the way a lawyer interrogates a witness, by means of simple yes-or-no questions, we should not be surprised that the answers come in discrete chunks. Because there is a finest grain to information there has to be a finest grain to our experience of nature.

Chapter 3: RESPECTING NATURE

1. Quoted in *New Scientist,* 15 August 1998, p. 88.
2. Bill McKibben, *The End of Nature* (Viking, 1990).
3. Michael Freeman, *Railways and the Victorian Imagination* (Yale University Press, 1999) p. 38.
4. McKibben, op. cit. p. 54.
5. The passage is quoted from *The Prose of Rupert Brooke* (1956) in John Grigg, *The Young Lloyd George* (Methuen, 1973) p. 253. Lloyd George himself had visited the Rockies in 1899, but his reaction was very different. Grigg comments, 'He could do without ghosts as cheerfully as he could do without gods.'
6. Seamus Heaney, *New Selected Poems* (Faber and Faber, 1990) p. 3.
7. The story of these changes of perception has been frequently told. Keith Thomas, *Man and the Natural World. Changing attitudes in England 1500–1800* (Allen Lane, 1983) provides a wonderfully panoramic and massively documented overview.

8. From *The Excursion*, Book 1.
9. Gerhard von Rad, *Old Testament Theology* (Oliver and Boyd, 1962) Volume 1, p. 27.
10. Hosea 2:5, 8; 4:13.
11. ibid. 11:1.
12. I Kings 19:12.
13. This was the theme of T. H. Huxley's Romanes Lecture of 1893.

> For his successful progress, throughout the savage state, man has been largely indebted to those qualities which he shares with the ape and the tiger ... after the manner of successful persons, civilized man would gladly kick down the ladder by which he has climbed. He would be only too pleased to see 'the ape and tiger' die. But they decline to suit his convenience ...

For useful modern discusssions see J. F. Haught, *God after Darwin. A Theology of Evolution* (Westview Press, 2000) Chapter 8 on 'Religion, Ethics and Evolution', and Michael Ruse, *Can a Darwinian be a Christian?* (Cambridge University Press, 2001) Chapter 10 on 'Social Darwinism'.
14. Francis Bacon, *Novum Organon*, 1620, Aphorism cxxix.
15. Henry Fielding, *The History and Adventures of Joseph Andrews, and of his Friend Mr Abraham Adams*, 1742.
16. Simon Schama, *Landscape and Memory* (HarperCollins, 1995).
17. A dramatised version of the incident is to be found in Roger Osborne, *The Floating Egg. Episodes in the Making of Geology* (Jonathan Cape, 1998) Chapter 4.
18. Genesis 2:19.
19. Edwin Muir, *One Foot in Eden* (Faber and Faber, 1965).
20. The concept of environmental niches has long been part of evolutionary theory. Different organisms survive by adapting themselves to different micro-environments. Human beings are unique in the extent to which we adapt our environment to suit ourselves, as for example, in building and heating houses. It is slowly being recognised, though, that other organisms may also actively influence their own evolution by restructuring their environmental niches for themselves and their descendants. It is an insight which adds a further dimension of fluidity to the concept of the environment.
21. John Passmore, *Man's Responsibility for Nature* (Duckworth, 1974). The question why we should feel obligations towards posterity is discussed in Chapter 4. His theory that our obligations depend on what we love is contested by Attfield. See note 24.
22. ibid. p. 182.
23. Edited by Norman Myers (Pan Books, 1985).
24. Robin Attfield, *The Ethics of Environmental Concern* (Blackwell, 1983). An influential development of the tradition of stewardship by a Christian philosopher.

25. Paul W. Taylor, *Respect for Nature. A Theory of Environmental Ethics* (Princeton, 1986). A philosophical defence of biocentricity, which spells out its practical implications.
26. Ruth Page, *God and the Web of Creation* (SCM, 1996).
27. Ruse, op. cit. p. 179.
28. Paul Colinvaux, *Why Big Fierce Animals are Rare* (Penguin, 1980). This must surely be one of the most entertaining popular books on ecology. But it has a sting in the tail. Human beings, in terms of what we do, must qualify as big and fierce. Unfortunately for the rest of nature, we are not rare.
29. Charles Taylor, *Philosophy and the Human Sciences* (Cambridge University Press, 1985) pp. 159–60. In an essay on Foucault, Taylor describes how the link between the domination of nature and the domination of man, as set out by Schiller, was unintentionally made more convincing by Foucault's analysis of the structures of control.
30. Jürgen Moltmann, *God in Creation. An ecological doctrine of creation* (SCM, 1985) p. 197.
31. ibid. p. 296.
32. Ronald H. Preston, *Confusions in Christian Social Ethics* (SCM, 1994).
33. R. John Elford and Ian S. Markham (Eds.), *The Middle Way. Theology, Politics and Economics in the later thought of R. H. Preston* (SCM, 2000) pp. 161 and 150ff.
34. David Gosling, *A New Earth* (CCBI, 1992). The author was for five years director of Church and Society in the WCC. The book gives a brief account of the kind of issues with which my committee was concerned.
35. This is the point finally reached by Kate Soper in *What is Nature?* (Blackwell, 1995). She approaches the topic from a totally secular, indeed anti-religious, point of view. She writes on p. 277:

    > What is really needed, one might argue, is not so much new forms of awe and reverence for nature, but rather to extend to it some of the more painful forms of concern we have for ourselves. The sense of rupture and distance that has been encouraged by secular rationality may be better overcome, not by worshipping this 'other' to humanity, but through a process of re-sensitization to our combined separation from it and dependence on it.

    It is the kind of statement which seems to me to hold out a prospect of useful dialogue.
36. Laurence Sterne, *The Life and Opinions of Tristram Shandy*, 1759. Penguin Classics Edn, p. 131.

Chapter 4: FOLLOWING NATURE

1. There is a useful summary of different concepts of 'species' in Ernst Mayr, *One Long Argument* (Penguin, 1991) Chapter 3.

2. E. O. Wilson, *Sociobiology: The New Synthesis* (Harvard University Press, 1975) and his *On Human Nature* (Harvard, 1978) are the classic texts. G. E. Pugh, *The Biological Origin of Human Values* (Routledge and Kegan Paul, 1978) gives an interestingly different account based on his work on 'value driven' decision systems.

3. C. T. Palmer and Randy Thornhill, *A Natural History of Rape: the Biological Basis of Sexual Coercion* (MIT, 2000).

4. *Times Higher Education Supplement*, 4 February 2000, p. 20.

5. See Chapter 2, p. 28ff.

6. Michael Ruse, *Can a Darwinian be a Christian?* (Cambridge University Press, 2001) p. 210. Mimicry has also been suggested as a reason for the evolution of human co-operation. *New Scientist*, 24 February 2001, p. 7.

7. Blaise Pascal, *Pensées* (Everyman Edn) 418.

8. I have explored these themes more fully in John Habgood, *Being a Person* (Hodder and Stoughton, 1998).

9. Basil Willey, *The English Moralists* (Chatto and Windus, 1964) Chapter 6 on '*Naturam Sequere*'.

10. Ray Monk, *Bertrand Russell. The Spirit of Solitude* (Jonathan Cape, 1996) *passim*.

11. Sophocles, *The Theban Plays*.

12. Romans 2:14–15.

13. Quoted in John Mahoney, *The Making of Moral Theology* (Clarendon Press, 1987) p. 79.

14. Alasdair Macintyre, *Whose Justice? Which Rationality?* (Duckworth, 1988) p. 197.

15. The point is made repeatedly in Michael Ignatieff's *Isaiah Berlin. A Life* (Chatto and Windus, 1998) e.g. on p. 89. Berlin went further in his more disputable claim that, whereas cultures may share similar prohibitions, they may differ fundamentally in those they uphold as virtues, p.285.

16. Joseph Butler, *Fifteen Sermons on Human Nature*, 1726, Sermon III.

17. D. M. Mackinnon, *A Study in Ethical Theory* (A. & C. Black, 1957) pp. 196–7.

18. David Hume, *A Treatise of Human Nature*, 1739, ed. L. A. Selby-Bigge (Oxford) p. 484.

19. Isaiah Berlin, *Against the Current*, ed. Henry Hardy (Pimlico, 1997) p. 1.

20. Edmund Burke, *Reflections on the Revolution in France*, 1790, ed. Conor Cruise O'Brien (Pelican Classics) pp. 152–3.

21. Macintyre, op. cit. p. 210.

22. Steven Mithen, *The Prehistory of the Mind* (Thames and Hudson, 1996) pp. 48–50. The anthropologist referred to is Hugh Brody whose book *Maps and Dreams* (Penguin, 1981) alternates between an insider's and an outsider's experience of the Beaver Indians.

23. Mary Midgley, *Beast and Man. The Roots of Human Nature* (Revised Edition (Routledge, 1995) pp. 259ff.
24. ibid. p. 280. Midgley's *The Ethical Primate. Humans, freedom and morality* (Routledge, 1994) is also highly relevant to this theme.
25. C. S. Lewis, *The Abolition of Man. Reflections on education with special reference to the teaching of English in the upper forms of schools* (Geoffrey Bles, 1943).
26. John Finnis, *Natural Law and Natural Rights* (Clarendon Press, 1980) pp. 86–90.
27. *New Scientist*, 9 June 2001, pp. 27–9.
28. Rowan Williams, *Lost Icons. Reflections on Cultural Bereavement* (T & T Clark, 2000) p. 57. Williams also has a useful description of 'fraternity' as 'a sense of integration, of belonging with an entire social body extending far beyond one's choice or one's affiliations of interest and "natural" loyalty', p. 54.
29. Michel de Montaigne, *Essays*, 1580. Book 1 no. 50.
30. The relation between play and sport is complex and subtle, and by no means all as negative as my comment on commercial sport implies. There is a story about an Oxford student who, when asked for an essay on the difference between them, wrote the single sentence, 'to play with Amaryllis in the shade would be unkind'. It was a brilliant answer, echoing of course Milton's lines in 'Lycidas':

> Were it not better done, as others use,
> To sport with Amaryllis in the shade,
> Or with the tangles of Neaera's hair?

The true character of play would seem to lie somewhere between the over-seriousness condemned by Montaigne, and the lack of seriousness identified by the student.
31. Mithen, op. cit. pp. 154ff.
32. Christopher Wills, *The Runaway Brain. The Evolution of Human Uniqueness* (Flamingo, 1995) p. 108.
33. Most of us can recognise a game when we see one, yet as Wittgenstein famously pointed out (*Philosophical Investigations*, 66–71) there is nothing common to all games – only family resemblances. The same might be said of art.
34. Genesis 1:27.
35. 'He who would do good to another must do it in Minute Particulars' from Blake's 'Jerusalem'.
36. Pascal Boyer's *Religion Explained. The human instincts that fashion gods, spirits and ancestors* (William Heinnemann, 2001) may be less than convincing as a total 'explanation', but makes a good case for holding that the mental systems and predispositions undergirding religious experience are indeed universal.
37. I owe these suggestions to a former colleague, Leslie Paul. His books *Nature into History* (Faber and Faber, 1957) and *Coming to Terms*

with Sex (Collins, 1969) are both relevant to the theme, but never had the attention which I think they deserved. A contemporary account of initiation ceremonies by Pascal Boyer (see note 36) lays similar stress on their socialising effect. Boys will turn into men whether the ceremonies are performed or not, but rituals which test endurance, loyalty, and a willingness to undergo humiliation, can play a major part in building up mutual trust for the future. Boys enter their adult role as members of a co-operative who have shared their supposed secrets and their suffering.

38. Michel Foucault, *The History of Sexuality*, Volume I, 1976, which deals at length with the hypothesis of domination and repression.

39. Charles Taylor, *Philosophy and the Human Sciences* (Cambridge University Press, 1985) Chapter 6 on 'Foucault on Freedom and Truth'.

40. Jeremiah 5:8.

41. L. William Countryman, *Dirt, Greed & Sex. Sexual Ethics in the New Testament and their Implications for Today* (SCM Press, 1988).

42. Kaye Wellings et. al., *Sexual Behaviour in Britain. The National Survey of Sexual Attitudes and Lifestyles* (Penguin, 1994) p. 227.

43. Countryman, op. cit., has much useful material on this point. The literature on homosexuality is, of course, immense, but it has not been my purpose to go further into the subject, than to point out the ambivalences inherent in any appeal to 'nature'.

Chapter 5: IMPROVING NATURE

1. Steven Mithen, *The Prehistory of the Mind* (Thames and Hudson, 1996) pp. 17–32, contain a useful summary of the different types of artefacts which can be matched with different stages of mental development.

2. Edmund Leach, *Lévi-Strauss* (Fontana, 1970) pp. 29–35.

3. Robert Temple, *The Genius of China* (Prion, 1998) p. 15.

4. *New Scientist*, 10 March 2001, p. 12.

5. It was precisely awareness of this set of difficulties which led the government of the day to set up the 'Human Fertilisation and Embryology Authority' in 1990 with power to oversee *in vitro* fertilisation, and to authorise, or rule out, particular types of research within a broad legal framework. The decisions made by an Authority can be much more carefully and sensitively attuned to particular circumstances than a law, especially during a period of rapid change.

6. *New Scientist*, 31 October 1998, p. 56. This issue also contains a long and informative series of articles on 'Living in a GM World'.

7. Robert Shapiro, *The Human Blueprint* (St Martin's Press, 1991). Among many other books on the same subject Michael J. Reiss and Roger Straughan, *Improving Nature? The science and ethics of genetic engineering* (Cambridge University Press, 1996) provides an excellent introduction to the whole field. Pete Moore, *Babel's Shadow. Genetic*

technologies in a fracturing society (Lion Publishing, 2000) covers the same ground in a racier journalistic style. Both books bring Christian insights to bear on the issues.

8. The technology is too recent to have received much attention in books for general readers. Moore, op. cit., has a brief mention. A Department of Health Report, *Stem Cell Research: Medical Progress with Responsibility*, June 2000, provides a clear account of the technology itself and some of its ethical implications.

9. See note 8.

10. Andrew Kimbrell, *The Human Body Shop. The Engineering and Marketing of Life* (HarperCollins, 1993) is an early, but still relevant, critique of the commodification of human life, especially in the USA.

11. Pete Moore, op. cit. p. 187.

12. This is the hypothesis proposed by James Lovelock in *Gaia: A New Look at Life on Earth* (Oxford University Press, 1982) in which the earth itself is treated as if it were a self-correcting, self-sustaining organism. Some systems, e.g. the atmosphere in its relation to the oceans, do seem to behave in this way. But the hypothesis remains highly controversial.

13. The phenomenon, known as apomixis, is described in *New Scientist*, 28 October 2000, p. 5.

14. It first became possible to 'engineer' genes in 1973. This led to a self-imposed moratorium until 1975, while the safety implications were considered. The first successful *in vitro* fertilisation took place in 1979, thus creating the conditions for genetic manipulation in humans. In the same year the implications of the new technology were discussed, among many other topics, at a major world conference of scientists and theologians, held at the Massachusetts Institute of Technology under the auspices of the World Council of Churches. The report of the conference was published in 1980 under the title *Faith and Science in an Unjust World*. A much briefer report, *Manipulating Life. Ethical issues in genetic engineering*, was published by a WCC working party in 1982. In the intervening years the social problems have not diminished. In 1995 a lecturer, Christopher Haskins, listed 'the vested interests in the food game' as devious governments, the neurotic middle-classes, the campaigning aristocracy, unscrupulous farmers, evangelistic organics, self-righteous environmentalists, lethal animal lovers, dogmatic scientists, pompous journalists, and greedy company chairmen. It may have been a bit unfair, but it was a useful reminder that those responsible for our food supply have to deal with more than one set of difficult people.

15. *New Scientist*, 25 November 2000, pp. 16–17.

16. *New Scientist*, 3 February 2001, pp. 16–17.

17. David L. Gosling, *Religion and Ecology in India and Southeast Asia* (Routledge, 2001) p. 19.

18. Genesis 3:5 describes the temptation to 'be like God', but in Genesis 1:27 it has already been declared that human beings are created in God's own image. I used the two texts as the basis for a sermon to the conference referred to in note 14. It ended with the words:

> The bigger the conference, the longer the years of preparation, the more intense the efforts, the more generous the supplies of scholarship, the more conscious we are of our ultimate inadequacy. But it is just then, in the failure of our godlikeness, that we can dare to go to the man on the cross. 'Would you be like God?' he asks us. 'Then you can attain it only by sharing the pain and the darkness, the self-giving and the self-restraint, of God's way of being God.'

The whole sermon is to be found in John Habgood, *A Working Faith* (Darton, Longman and Todd, 1980) pp. 52–7. The reference to unused talents is in Matthew 25:24–30.

19. From Tennyson's 'In Memoriam'.

20. The revival of 'natural' landscapes in the eighteenth century was largely the work of Capability Brown, who earned his nickname by his skill in drawing out the countryside's 'capabilities', rather than imposing on it the highly formalised and artificial constructions which were then in fashion.

21. John Brooke and Geoffrey Cantor, *Reconstructing Nature. The Engagement of Science and Religion* (T & T Clark, 1998) p. 319.

Chapter 6: NATURE'S GOD

1. Alan Bennett, *Telling Tales* (BBC, 2000) p. 66.
2. Karen Armstrong, *The Battle for God. Fundamentalism in Judaism, Christianity and Islam* (HarperCollins, 2000) p. 369.
3. Special Report on 'Creationism' in *New Scientist*, 22 April 2000, pp. 33–48.
4. *Journal of Biological Education* (2000), 34(3) pp. 139–46.
5. That misguided attempts to prove the existence of God from the study of nature can result in atheism, is the main theme of Michael J. Buckley's *At the Origins of Modern Atheism* (Yale University Press, 1987). See also Chapter 3 of my *Varieties of Unbelief* (Darton, Longman and Todd, 2000) and Austin Farrer, *Faith and Speculation* (A. & C. Black, 1967) especially Chapter 1.
6. Ludwig Wittgenstein, *Culture and Value* (Revised Edn, Blackwell, 1998) p. 97e.
7. Paul Tillich, *Theology of Culture* (Oxford University Press, 1959) p. 13.
8. Karl Rahner, *Foundations of Christian Faith* (Darton, Longman and Todd, 1978) p. 52. The point is made more fully in *Theological Investigations* (Darton, Longman and Todd, 1979) Volume 16, p. 14:

> The act whereby personal existence is accepted in trust and hope is

therefore, as long as it is not the victim of self-deception, a letting go of oneself into the incomprehensible mystery. Christianity is far from being a clarification of the world and existence; rather it contains the prohibition against treating any experience or insight, however illuminating it may be, as conclusive and intelligible in itself. Christians have less answers (at their disposal) than other mortals to hand out with a 'now everything is clear'. A Christian cannot enter God as an obvious item in the balance sheet of life; he can only accept him as an incomprehensible mystery in silence and adoration, as the beginning and end of his hope and therefore as his unique, ultimate and all-embracing salvation.

9. This was a constant theme in his writings. See for example Ian T. Ramsey, *Religious Language. An Empirical Placing of Theological Phrases* (SCM Press, 1957).

10. This is a further consequence of Gödel's Incompleteness Theorem, referred to in Chapter 2, note 30. The idea of tacit knowledge is a major theme of Michael Polanyi's *Personal Knowledge* (Routledge and Kegan Paul, 1958).

11. Psalm 34:8.

12. See, for example, the chapter on 'Theological Integrity' in Rowan Williams, *On Christian Theology* (Blackwell, 2000).

13. ibid. Chapter 5 'On Being Creatures'.

14. Donald Mackinnon, *Borderlands of Theology* (Lutterworth, 1968) p. 79. See also Chapter 5 note 18, and Williams, op. cit., p. 161.

15. This is a theme closely linked with 'play' as discussed in Chapter 4 of this book. As in that chapter, I am indebted to Rowan Williams, *Lost Icons* (T & T Clark, 2000). John Habgood, *Being a Person* (Hodder and Stoughton, 1998) Chapter 10 approaches the same conclusion from a different angle.

16. Rowan Williams, *On Christian Theology*, op. cit. p. 83.

17. Teilhard de Chardin, *The Phenomenon of Man* (Collins, 1959) p. 110. It is a pity he went on to spoil a good metaphor by describing groping as directed chance. That misses the point. The essence of groping is that it is blind, but there needs to be some way of knowing when it has found something useful.

18. There is a simple, non-technical exploration of all these themes in Michael Ruse, *Can a Darwinian be a Christian?* (Cambridge University Press, 2000). For a discussion of direction in evolution see pp. 84-93.

19. David Hay, *Exploring Inner Space. Is God still possible in the twentieth century?* (Mowbray, 1987) and *Religious Experience Today. Studying the Facts* (Mowbray, 1990). Both books have interesting things to say about the tendency of many people who undergo religious experience to discount it and keep it to themselves, because they have no adequate symbolism in which to express it.

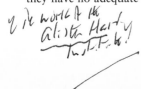

[183]

20. *Revelations of Divine Love*, 1373. Chapter 5.
21. John Oman, *The Natural and the Supernatural* (Cambridge University Press, 1931) p. 71.
22. ibid. p. 210.
23. Ruse, op. cit. p. 149. The quotation is all the more interesting in that Ruse does not himself appear to profess any religious belief.
24. *New Scientist*, 24 March 2001, pp. 29–30.
25. James A. Carpenter, *Nature and Grace. Towards an Integral Perspective* (Crossroad, 1988) p. 1.
26. John Mahoney, *The Making of Moral Theology. A Study of Roman Catholic Tradition* (Clarendon Press, 1987) p. 84.
27. Anthony Meredith, *Gregory of Nyssa* (Routledge, 1999) p. 24.
28. Carpenter, op. cit. p. 30.
29. Karl Rahner, *Nature and Grace* (Sheed and Ward, 1963). This and the following quotations are on pp. 36, 35 and 41.
30. Ephesians 6:12.
31. Stanley L. Jaki, *Science and Creation* (Scottish Academic Press, 1986) p. 262.
32. The point is disputed, but has been vigorously defended by Jaki, op. cit. Chapter 12.
33. James Lovelock's Gaia hypothesis, referred to in Chapter 5 note 12, can be interpreted as a move in this direction.
34. R. S. Thomas, 'The Bright Field', from *Later Poems 1972–1982* (Macmillan, 1983).

INDEX